Contents

Section 1: Introduction

1.1 Scope

This guide provides detailed guidance for the installation of fixed building services in new and existing non-domestic buildings to help compliance with the energy efficiency requirements of the Building Regulations.

This edition covers the design, installation and commissioning of:

- conventional means of providing primary space heating, domestic hot water, mechanical ventilation, comfort cooling and interior lighting
- low carbon generation of heat by heat pumps and combined heat and power systems.

The guide sets out recommended minimum energy efficiency standards for components of building services systems, including the use of controls. For systems installed in new buildings, the standards are design limits (or backstop values). For new or replacement systems and components installed in existing buildings, the standards represent reasonable provision for complying with the Building Regulations.

It is important to note that standards higher than many of these recommended minimum standards will need to be achieved if:

- new buildings are to meet the the Building Regulations target carbon dioxide emission rate (TER) calculated using National Calculation Methodology (NCM) tools such as SBEM[1]
- systems (up to 45 kW heat output) are to comply with the Microgeneration Certification Scheme standards that enable building owners to receive payments under the Renewable Heat Incentive (RHI) and qualify for Green Deal funding
- products are to be recognised as renewable technologies under the Renewable Energy Directive.

The guide includes some supplementary information that identifies good practice design and installation standards that exceed the minimum standards in this guide. Microgeneration Certification Scheme standards[2] are an example of good practice standards.

In relevant sections, the guide identifies additional non-prescriptive measures (for example additional controls) that can improve plant efficiency. These may be used to gain 'heating efficiency credits' to help meet the carbon dioxide emission targets for new buildings, or the recommended minimum energy efficiency standards set out in this guide for work in existing buildings.

A summary of recommended minimum energy efficiency standards is presented in Table 1 at the end of this section.

---

1   The National Calculation Methodology (NCM) modelling guide and the Simplified Building Energy Model (SBEM) tool can be downloaded from www.ncm.bre.co.uk.
2   http://www.microgenerationcertification.org/mcs-standards

1.2 Innovative systems

It is also important to note that this guide covers a range of frequently occurring situations. It deals with the most commonly used fixed building services technologies. In doing so it neither endorses these methods and technologies nor excludes other more innovative technologies that may offer an alternative means of meeting the functional requirements of the Building Regulations.

Where the alternative technology has been the subject of a recognised testing procedure that assesses its energy performance, this may be used to indicate that the system is adequately efficient. In the event that there is no recognised testing standard, suitable calculations or modelling methods may be used to show the carbon performance of the system.

1.3 European directives

The design and installation of fixed building services products, such as boilers, circulators and heat pumps, shall at the appropriate time comply with all relevant requirements of EU directives as implemented in the United Kingdom. There are a number of directives with requirements that directly or indirectly control the energy efficiency of building services.

The **Ecodesign Directive 2009/125/EC** provides a framework for establishing requirements for 'energy-related' products placed on the EU market. Current requirements cover 'energy-using' products such as boilers, light bulbs and washing machines. In the future, requirements will also cover products such as windows, insulation material and shower heads whose use has an impact on energy consumption.

The requirements are set out in Commission Regulations listed in the document http://ec.europa.eu/energy/efficiency/ecodesign/doc/overview_legislation_eco-design.pdf. Products covered by the regulations can only be CE marked and placed on the market if they meet the ecodesign standards specified.

At the time of preparation of this guide, Commission Regulations existed or were being developed for:

- space heaters and combination heaters
- water heaters and hot water storage tanks
- glandless standalone circulators and glandless circulators integrated in products
- water pumps
- air conditioners and comfort fans
- fans driven by motors with an electric input power between 125 W and 500 kW
- lighting products in the domestic and tertiary sectors
- electric motors.

The intention is that the recommended minimum product standards in this guide should at least match the energy efficiency standards set out in Commission Regulations *as they come into force*. For example, although the implementing regulations for hot water storage tanks were published in September 2013, the standards do not come into force until September 2017.

If in any doubt as to whether a product is subject to minimum ecodesign standards, check the Commission document above.

The **Energy Labelling Directive 2010/30/EU** complements the Ecodesign Directive by providing a framework for labelling of energy-related products including lamps, luminaires, household air conditioners and washing machines. The Energy Label classifies products on an A to G scale, 'pulling' the market towards more efficient products by better informing consumers. The Ecodesign Directive, by contrast, uses regulation to 'push' the market away from the worst performing products.

The **Renewable Energy Directive 2009/28/EC** provides a framework for the promotion of energy from renewable resources. It sets a mandatory UK target of 15% energy generation from renewable sources by 2020 – the 'renewable energy obligation' – as a contribution to meeting the EU's overall target of 20%. Of relevance to building services is that it includes criteria for training and certification of installers of renewables. The directive also specifies in Annex VII the standards that heat pumps must achieve to be recognised as renewable technologies by the directive.

The **Energy Efficiency Directive 2012/27/EU** establishes a common framework of measures for the promotion of energy efficiency within the EU in order to ensure that the EU meets its target of a 20% reduction in primary energy consumption by 2020. Legislation to implement the directive in the UK will be published by 5 June 2014. Included will be requirements for public authorities to purchase only energy-efficient products, services and buildings; and requirements for heat meters to be fitted in apartments and buildings connected to a central source of heating or district heating network. For more information on the specific requirements and technical standards, see the DECC website[3].

The **Energy Performance of Buildings Directive 2010/31/EU** is a recast of the original 2002/91/EC directive, which in 2002 introduced requirements for:

- the establishment of a methodology for calculating the integrated energy performance of buildings

- minimum energy performance requirements for new buildings, and, where feasible, for larger buildings undergoing major renovation

- energy performance certification of buildings, and

- inspections of heating and air conditioning systems.

The recast directive includes a new requirement to consider, in the design of new buildings, the feasibility of using renewables and other 'high-efficiency alternative systems'. There is no mandatory format for this assessment, but it will now be necessary to declare (through a new field in the energy performance calculation software) that it has been carried out.

The Building Regulations, which already met the original requirements in many ways (for example by setting standards for new buildings), have been amended in some places to reflect the new requirements of the directive. For guidance on the changes affecting new buildings, see Approved Document L2A. For guidance on the changes affecting major renovations, see Approved Document L2B. For guidance on other requirements relating to building certification and inspection of heating and air conditioning systems, see the DCLG website[4].

1.4 Status of guide

The Building Regulations contain functional requirements, such as requirements that buildings must be structurally stable, constructed and fitted to ensure fire protection, and energy efficient. These functional requirements are often drafted in broad terms, and so it may not always be immediately clear to a person carrying out work how to comply with the relevant requirements. Consequently, the Department for Communities and Local Government issues documents, known as approved documents, which provide practical guidance on ways of complying with specific aspects of the Building Regulations in some of the more common building situations.

Approved documents are not always comprehensive and may contain references to other documents which will provide more detailed information and assistance on parts of the guidance. This guide is one of those documents: it provides more detailed information on the guidance contained in Approved

3 https://www.gov.uk/decc
4 https://www.gov.uk/dclg

Documents L2A and L2B about compliance with the energy efficiency requirements which apply when installing fixed building services in new and existing buildings.

If you follow the relevant guidance in an approved document, and in any document referred to in the approved document (such as this guide) which provides additional information to help you follow that guidance, there is a legal presumption that you have complied with the Building Regulations. However, in each case it is for the building control body (local authority or approved inspector) to decide whether work complies with the requirements of the Building Regulations. It is therefore sensible that you check with the building control body before starting work what they consider it is necessary for you to do to comply with the requirements of the Building Regulations.

1.5 How to use this guide

The guide is divided into the following sections:

Section 1: Introduction and summary of energy efficiency standards

Section 2: Gas, oil and biomass-fired boilers

Section 3: Heat pumps

Section 4: Gas and oil-fired warm air heaters

Section 5: Gas and oil-fired radiant heaters

Section 6: Combined heat and power and community heating

Section 7: Direct electric space heating

Section 8: Domestic hot water

Section 9: Comfort cooling

Section 10: Air distribution

Section 11: Pipework and ductwork insulation

Section 12: Lighting

Section 13: Heating and cooling system circulators and water pumps

Supplementary information is shown against a blue background. This may be further information to help with interpreting the minimum energy efficiency provisions needed to comply with the Building Regulations. Or it may be guidance on best practice that goes beyond the recommended minimum standards.

Key terms are printed in blue and are defined at appropriate points throughout the guide.

1.6 Key terms for space heating and domestic hot water systems

The following general definitions are applicable to the sections that deal with space heating and hot water. Further definitions are included in later sections as appropriate.

Heat generator means a device for converting fuel or electricity into heat – e.g. a boiler or radiant heater.

Heat generator efficiency means the useful heat output divided by the energy input in the fuel (based on gross calorific value) or electricity delivered to the heat generator, as determined by the appropriate test methods for that type of heat generator.

Heat generator seasonal efficiency means the estimated seasonal heat output from the heat generator divided by the energy input. This will depend on the heat generator efficiency and the operating mode of the heat generator over the heating season. For example, in the case of boilers it is a 'weighted' average of the efficiencies of the boiler at 30% and 100% of the boiler output. For other technologies the heat generator seasonal efficiency may be the same as the heat generator efficiency.

Minimum controls package means a package of controls specific to each technology that represents the recommended minimum provision necessary to meet the Building Regulations energy efficiency requirements.

Additional measures means additional controls or other measures that go beyond the recommended minimum controls package and for which heating efficiency credits are available.

Heating efficiency credits are awarded for the provision of additional measures, such as additional controls, that raise the energy efficiency of the system and go beyond recommended minimum standards. Different credits apply to the different measures that are available for heating and hot water technologies.

Effective heat generator seasonal efficiency is obtained by adding heating efficiency credits, where applicable, to the heat generator seasonal efficiency:

Effective heat generator seasonal efficiency =
heat generator seasonal efficiency + heating efficiency credits   **Equation 1**

Where relevant, this guide sets standards for effective heat generator seasonal efficiency so that a heat generator with an inherently low efficiency may be used in combination with additional measures.

Space heating system means the complete system that is installed to provide heating to the space. It includes the heating plant and the distribution system by which heating is delivered to zones. Heat losses from the distribution system can be addressed by reference to guidance by TIMSA on HVAC insulation[5].

Domestic hot water system means a local or central system for providing hot water for use by building occupants.

1.7 Summary of recommended minimum energy efficiency standards

Unless specified otherwise in this guide, it is recommended that, where applicable, building services are provided with controls that as a minimum correspond to Band C in BS EN 15232:2012 *Energy performance of buildings. Impact of building automation, controls and building management.*

---

5   TIMSA *HVAC guidance for achieving compliance with Part L of the Building Regulations* at www.timsa.org.uk

Table 1 Recommended minimum energy efficiency standards for building services[6]

Gas, oil and biomass-fired boilers: new buildings		Seasonal efficiency (gross[7])
Natural gas	Single-boiler system ≤ 2 MW output	91%
	Single-boiler system > 2 MW output	86%
	Multiple-boiler system	82% for any individual boiler 86% for overall multi-boiler system
LPG	Single-boiler system ≤ 2 MW output	93%
	Single-boiler system > 2 MW output	87%
	Multiple-boiler system	82% for any individual boiler 87% for overall multi-boiler system
Oil	Single-boiler system	84%
	Multiple-boiler system	82% for any individual boiler 84% for overall multi-boiler system
Biomass – independent, automatic, pellet/woodchip		75%

Gas, oil and biomass-fired boilers: existing buildings	Seasonal efficiency (gross)	
	Actual	Effective
Natural gas	82%	84%
LPG	83%	85%
Oil	84%	86%
Biomass – independent, automatic, pellet/woodchip		75%

Heat pump units		Coefficient of performance (COP)
Air-to-air	Space heating ≤ 12 kW	Seasonal COP 'D' rating for median temperature range in BS EN 14825[8]
All others except absorption and gas-engine	Space heating	2.5 (250%) at rating conditions in BS EN 14511[9]
	Domestic hot water	2.0 (200%) at rating conditions in BS EN 14511
Absorption		0.5 (50%) when operating at the rating conditions
Gas-engine		1.0 (100%) when operating at the rating conditions

6   Emerging European regulations implementing the Ecodesign Directive set minimum standards for the efficiency of energy-using products that can be placed on the market. Products should also comply with these standards as they come into effect. Current regulations are listed at http://ec.europa.eu/energy/efficiency/ecodesign/doc/overview_legislation_eco-design.pdf.

7   Efficiency is heat output divided by calorific value of fuel. The net calorific value of a fuel excludes the latent heat of water vapour in the exhaust, and so is lower than the gross calorific value. Efficiency test results and European standards normally use net calorific values.

8   Seasonal coefficient of performance (SCOP) is the current Ecodesign Directive measure for space heating air-to-air heat pumps with an output of up to 12 kW. Eventually, the measure used will be the seasonal primary energy efficiency ratio (SPEER), with testing and rating to BS EN 14825:2013 *Air conditioners, liquid chilling packages and heat pumps with electrically driven compressors for space heating and cooling. Testing and rating at part load conditions and calculation of seasonal performance.* Energy labelling with the SPEER rating will be mandatory from 2015.

9   Rating conditions are standardised conditions provided for the determination of data presented in BS EN 14511:2013 *Air conditioners, liquid chilling packages and heat pumps with electrically driven compressors for space heating and cooling.*

Table 1 Recommended minimum energy efficiency standards for building services (continued)

Gas and oil-fired warm air systems	Thermal efficiency (net)	
Gas-fired forced convection (natural gas)	91%	
Gas-fired forced convection (LPG)	91%	
Direct gas-fired forced convection	100%	
Oil-fired forced convection	91%	

Radiant heaters	Efficiency (net)	
	Thermal	Radiant
Luminous radiant heater (unflued)	86%	55%
Non-luminous radiant heater (unflued)	86%	55%
Non-luminous radiant heater (flued)	86%	55%
Multi-burner radiant heater	91%	N/A

Combined heat and power (CHP)	CHPQA quality index	Power efficiency
All types	105	20%

Electric (primary) heating	Seasonal efficiency
Boiler and warm air	N/A

Domestic hot water systems		Heat generator seasonal efficiency (gross)	
		Thermal efficiency	Boiler seasonal efficiency
Direct-fired: new buildings	Natural gas > 30 kW output	90%	
	Natural gas ≤ 30 kW output	73%	
	LPG > 30 kW output	92%	
	LPG ≤ 30 kW output	74%	
	Oil	76%	
Direct-fired: existing buildings	Natural gas	73%	
	LPG	74%	
	Oil	75%	
Indirect-fired (dedicated hot water boiler)*: new and existing buildings	Natural gas		80%
	LPG		81%
	Oil		82%

*See Table 26 for method of calculating efficiency for primary return temperatures > or ≤ 55°C.

Electrically-heated: new and existing buildings	N/A

Table 1 Recommended minimum energy efficiency standards for building services *(continued)*

Comfort cooling systems	Energy efficiency ratio (EER)	
Packaged air conditioners – single-duct types	2.6	
Packaged air conditioners – other types	2.6	
Split and multi-split air conditioners > 12 kW	2.6	
Split and multi-split air conditioners ≤ 12 kW	SCOP 'D' rating for median temperature range in BS EN 14825	
Variable refrigerant flow systems	2.6	
Vapour compression cycle chillers, water cooled ≤ 750 kW	3.9	
Vapour compression cycle chillers, water cooled > 750 kW	4.7	
Vapour compression cycle chillers, air cooled ≤ 750 kW	2.55	
Vapour compression cycle chillers, air cooled > 750 kW	2.65	
Water loop heat pump	3.2	
Absorption cycle chillers	0.7	
Gas-engine-driven variable refrigerant flow	1.0	

Air distribution systems	Specific fan power (SFP)[10] (W/(l·s))	
	New buildings	Existing buildings
Central balanced mechanical ventilation system with heating and cooling	1.6	2.2
Central balanced mechanical ventilation system with heating only	1.5	1.8
All other central balanced mechanical ventilation systems	1.1	1.6
Zonal supply system where fan is remote from zone, such as ceiling void or roof-mounted units	1.1	1.4
Zonal extract system where fan is remote from zone	0.5	0.5
Zonal supply and extract ventilation units, such as ceiling void or roof units serving a single room or zone with heating and heat recovery	1.9	1.9
Local balanced supply and extract ventilation system, such as wall/roof units serving single area with heating and heat recovery	1.6	1.6
Local supply or extract ventilation units such as window/wall/roof units serving single area (e.g. toilet extract)	0.3	0.4
Other local ventilation supply or extract units	0.5	0.5
Fan-assisted terminal VAV unit	1.1	1.1
Fan coil units (rating weighted average)	0.5	0.5
Kitchen extract, fan remote from zone with grease filter	1.0	1.0

10   Maximum pressure drop is not specified.

Table 1 Recommended minimum energy efficiency standards for building services *(continued)*

Air distribution systems: new and existing buildings	Dry heat recovery efficiency
Plate heat exchanger	50%
Heat pipes	60%
Thermal wheel	65%
Run around coil	45%
Internal lighting: option 1	**Effective lighting efficacy**
General lighting in office, storage and industrial areas	60 luminaire lumens per circuit-watt
General lighting in other types of space	60 lamp lumens per circuit-watt
Display lighting	22 lamp lumens per circuit-watt
Internal lighting: option 2	**Lighting Energy Numeric Indicator (LENI)**
Lighting system	$\leq$ lighting energy limit (kWh/m^2/year) specified in Table 44
Heating system circulators and water pumps	**Energy Efficiency Index**
Glandless standalone circulators Glandless, standalone and integrated circulators	$\leq$ 0.27 until 31 July 2015 $\leq$ 0.23 from 1 August 2015
Water pumps	See Section 13

Section 2: Gas, oil and biomass-fired boilers

2.1 Introduction

This section provides guidance on specifying gas, oil and biomass-fired space heating systems for new and existing buildings to meet relevant energy efficiency requirements in the Building Regulations. It covers relevant boiler types, and describes measures, such as additional controls, that can be used to gain heating efficiency credits to improve the heat generator seasonal efficiency.

2.2 Scope of guidance

The guidance applies to wet central heating systems using commercial boilers fired by:

- natural gas

- liquid petroleum gas (LPG)

- oil, and

- biomass.

The guidance in this section does not cover:

- steam boilers (as these are used primarily for processes rather than provision of space heating), or

- electric boilers (for which see Section 7).

2.3 Key terms

The terminology used to describe efficiencies for boiler systems is detailed below. In this section the heat generator is a boiler.

Biomass means all material of biological origin, excluding material embedded in geological formations and transformed to fossil fuel.

Boiler efficiency means the energy delivered by the water as it leaves the boiler (or boilers in multi-boiler installations) to supply the heat emitters, divided by the energy (based on gross calorific value) in the fuel delivered to the boiler, expressed as a percentage. It is an expression of the boiler's performance and excludes energy used by boiler auxiliary controls, pumps, boiler room ventilation fans, mechanical flue extraction fans and fan dilution systems. The boiler efficiency is measured according to the standards that are used to demonstrate compliance with the Boiler Efficiency Directive[11].

Effective boiler seasonal efficiency is the boiler seasonal efficiency (as calculated by Equation 2 below for individual boilers, or by Equation 3.1 for multiple boilers), plus any applicable heating efficiency credits.

Economiser means a device, including a secondary heat exchanger fitted on or near to a boiler, which provides additional heat transfer capacity. For the purposes of this guide, any boiler which will be supplied with an economiser should have the economiser fitted when the boiler efficiency is tested according to the standards that are used to demonstrate compliance with the Boiler Efficiency Directive. The effect of this on the boiler efficiency at 30% and 100% of the boiler output may be taken into

---

11 Council Directive 92/42/EEC (the Boiler Efficiency Directive) relates to the efficiency requirements for new hot water boilers fired with liquid or gaseous fuels. The associated UK legislation is the Boiler (Efficiency) Regulations 1993 (SI 1993/3083), amended by the Boiler (Efficiency) (Amendment) Regulations 1994 (SI 1994/3083).

account in the values used for the calculation of the boiler seasonal efficiency using Equations 2 or 3.1, or the three-step method and Equations 3.2 and 3.3, as appropriate.

Condensing boiler means a boiler that offers a higher energy efficiency by recovering heat from the flue gases. This is achieved by increasing the heat exchanger surface area, which recovers extra sensible heat whenever the boiler fires. The boiler becomes even more efficient when system water temperatures are low because the larger heat exchanger area promotes condensation, allowing much of the latent heat to be recaptured. Standing losses (when the boiler is not firing) are low, and part load performance is very good. In multiple-boiler systems, condensing boilers can be used as the lead boiler.

Standard boiler means, in the context of this document, a non-condensing boiler.

Zone control means independent control of rooms or areas within buildings that need to be heated to different temperatures at different times. Where several rooms or areas of a building behave in a similar manner, they can be grouped together as a 'zone' and put on the same circuit and controller.

Sequence control enables two or more heating boilers to be switched on or off in sequence when the heating load changes. This maximises the efficiency of the boilers, so reducing fuel consumption, and reduces wear and tear on the boilers.

Direct acting weather compensation is a type of control that enables a heat generator to work at its optimum efficiency. The control allows the boiler to vary its operating flow temperature to suit the external temperature conditions and the temperatures inside the building. Weather compensation relies on communication between an external sensor and one inside the boiler. The boiler's water flow temperature is varied accordingly, so that energy is not wasted by the boiler turning on and off.

Weather compensation via a mixing valve is similar to direct acting weather compensation, except that the outside temperature is used to control the temperature of water supplied to the heat emitters by mixing the boiler flow and return rather than by altering the boiler temperature.

Optimum start is a control system or algorithm which starts plant operation at the latest time possible to achieve specified conditions at the start of the occupancy period.

Optimiser is a control system employing an optimum start algorithm.

Optimum stop is a control system or algorithm which stops plant operation at the earliest possible time such that internal conditions will not deteriorate beyond preset limits by the end of the occupancy period.

Two-stage burner control is a type of control that offers two distinct boiler firing rates.

Multi-stage burner control is a type of control that offers more than two distinct firing rates, but without continuous adjustment between firing rates.

Modulating burner control is a type of control that provides a continuously variable firing rate, which is altered to match the boiler load over the whole turndown ratio.

Decentralisation means the replacement of centralised boiler plant and its associated distribution pipework with several smaller, more accurately sized boiler plants, installed within or adjacent to the buildings or systems they serve. This eliminates long pipe runs between buildings or through unheated areas, so reducing heat losses.

Building management system (BMS) means a building-wide network which allows communication with and control of items of HVAC plant (and other building systems) from a single control centre, which may be local or remote. More advanced ('full') building management systems offer a wide range of functions, including sequential control, zone control, weather compensation, frost protection and night set-back, as well as monitoring and targeting.

2.4 Determining boiler seasonal efficiency

Single-boiler systems and multiple-boiler systems with identical boilers

For boilers the relevant heat generator seasonal efficiency is the boiler seasonal efficiency. The boiler seasonal efficiency is a 'weighted' average of the efficiencies of the boiler at 15%, 30% and 100% of the boiler output (the efficiency at 15% being taken to be the same as that at 30%). This is usually quoted by the boiler manufacturer. Note that the efficiencies based on net calorific value should be converted to efficiencies based on gross calorific value using the appropriate conversion factor in SAP 2012 Table E4.

The boiler efficiencies, measured at 100% load and at 30% load, are used in Equation 2 to calculate the boiler seasonal efficiency. The weighting factors in Equation 2 reflect typical seasonal operating conditions for a boiler.

$$\text{Boiler seasonal efficiency} = 0.81\eta_{30\%} + 0.19\eta_{100\%}$$

Equation 2[12]

where:

$\eta_{30\%}$ is the gross boiler efficiency measured at 30% load

$\eta_{100\%}$ is the gross boiler efficiency measured at 100% load.

Equation 2 applies to:

- single-boiler systems where the boiler output is $\leq$ 400 kW and the boiler will operate on a low temperature system

- multiple-boiler systems where all individual boilers have identical efficiencies and where the output of each boiler is $\leq$ 400 kW operating on low temperature systems.

For boilers with an output > 400 kW, the manufacturer's declared efficiencies should be used.

Multiple-boiler systems with non-identical boilers replacing existing systems

Where more than one boiler is installed on the same heating system and the efficiencies of the boilers are not all identical, Equation 3.1 should be used to calculate the overall boiler seasonal efficiency. All boilers should be included in the calculation, even when some are identical.

The boiler seasonal efficiency for multiple-boiler systems with non-identical boilers is:

$$\eta_{OBSE} = \frac{\Sigma(\eta_{BSE} \times R)}{\Sigma R}$$

Equation 3.1

where:

η_{OBSE} is the gross overall boiler seasonal efficiency, being an average weighted by boiler output of the individual seasonal boiler efficiencies

η_{BSE} is the gross boiler seasonal efficiency of each individual boiler calculated using Equation 2

R is the rated output in kW of each individual boiler (at 80/60°C).

---

12   This equation assumes that the efficiency at 15% load is the same as at 30% load (and the equation has been simplified accordingly).

Multiple-boiler systems in new buildings

In the case of multiple boilers in new buildings, the more accurate three-step method described below should be used to calculate the overall seasonal boiler efficiency. These steps can readily be programmed into a spreadsheet to automate the calculation.

Step 1

Determine the load on each boiler for each of the three system part-load conditions of 15%, 30% and 100%. For example, if the total system output is made up of three equally sized boilers, at 15% of system output the lead boiler will be operating at 45% of its rated output, with the other two boilers switched off.

Step 2

Determine the efficiency of each boiler for the above operating conditions. In the above example, the efficiency of the boiler operating at 45% can be determined by linear interpolation between its efficiencies at 30% and 100% of rated output. Where it is necessary to determine the efficiency of an individual boiler at 15% of rated output, this should be taken as the same as the efficiency at 30% of rated output. (Note that the efficiency at 15% of rated output will only be needed if a single boiler meets the full design output.)

Step 3

Calculate the overall operating efficiency at each of the system part load conditions using:

$$\eta_p = Q_p / \Sigma(q_{b,p}/\eta_{b,p})$$ **Equation 3.2**

where:

η_p is the system efficiency at part load condition p, i.e. 15%, 30% and 100% of system rated output

Q_p is the system heat output at part load condition p

$q_{b,p}$ is the individual boiler heat output at system part load condition p

$\eta_{b,p}$ is the individual boiler efficiency at system part load condition p.

Calculate the overall boiler seasonal efficiency as the weighted average of the efficiencies at the three load conditions using:

$$\eta_{OBSE} = 0.36\eta_{15\%} + 0.45\eta_{30\%} + 0.19\eta_{100\%}$$ **Equation 3.3**

Table 2 is a worksheet for following through these calculations (using manufacturer data for boiler efficiency at 100% and 30% output). Table 3 shows a completed example calculation using this worksheet, for the case where a system with a rated output of 625 kW is served by three boilers, each rated at 250 kW. The first two boilers are condensing boilers, while the third is a standard boiler. Because the installation is oversized (750 kW compared to 625 kW), at full system output the final boiler is only operating at 50% output (125/250).

The notes at the foot of the table illustrate how the various values are calculated.

Table 2 Worksheet for calculating the overall boiler seasonal efficiency of a multiple-boiler system using the alternative three-step method

Boiler no	Rating kW	Boiler % efficiency at boiler outputs of		Boiler % output at system outputs of			Boiler % efficiency at system outputs of		
		100%	30%	15%	30%	100%	15%	30%	100%
1									
2									
3									
System efficiency at part load									
Weighting factor							0.36	0.45	0.19
Overall heat generator seasonal efficiency									

Table 3 Example calculation of the overall boiler seasonal efficiency of a multiple-boiler system in a new building

Boiler no	Rating kW	Boiler % efficiency at boiler outputs of		Boiler % output at system outputs of			Boiler % efficiency at system outputs of		
		30%	100%	15%	30%	100%	15%	30%	100%
1	250	90%	86%	38.0%	75.0%	100.0%	89.6%[1]	87.4%	86.0%
2	250	90%	86%	not firing	not firing	100.0%	not firing	not firing	86.0%
3	250	85%	82%	not firing	not firing	50.0%	not firing	not firing	84.1%
System efficiency at part load							89.6%	87.4%	85.6%[2]
Weighting factor							0.36	0.45	0.19
Overall heat generator seasonal efficiency							87.9%[3]		

Notes

[1] Calculated by linear interpolation

$$\eta_{b,p} = \eta_{30\%} - (\eta_{30\%} - \eta_{100\%}) \times \frac{(q_{b,p} - 30\%)}{(100\% - 30\%)}$$

$$\eta_{1,15\%} = \eta_{30\%} - (\eta_{30\%} - \eta_{100\%}) \times \frac{(38\% - 30\%)}{(100\% - 30\%)}$$

[2] Calculated by dividing the thermal output of the system (625 kW) by the rate of fuel consumption, which is given by the sum of the boiler outputs divided by their individual operating efficiency, i.e.

$$\eta_{100\%} = \frac{625}{\dfrac{250 \times 100\%}{86.0\%} + \dfrac{250 \times 100\%}{86.0\%} + \dfrac{250 \times 50\%}{84.1\%}} = 85.6\%$$

[3] Calculated as the weighted average, i.e.

$$89.6\% \times 0.36 + 87.4\% \times 0.45 + 85.6\% \times 0.19 = 87.9\%$$

2.5 Boilers in new buildings

Background

New buildings should be provided with high efficiency condensing or non-condensing boilers that meet the recommended minimum standards for heat generator seasonal efficiency in this guide.

Commercial heating systems are inherently more complicated than domestic systems with a wider range of temperatures and heat emitters. The selection of condensing or non-condensing boilers will be determined by application and physical constraints.

Note: Water quality can have a major impact on system efficiency. It is important that designers take appropriate measures to ensure that the system water is of good quality.

Condensing boilers will meet projected efficiencies only when they operate with a system return temperature between 30°C and 40°C for 80% of the annual operating hours. With a return temperature of 55°C and above, condensing boilers will not produce condensate and will have similar efficiencies to non-condensing high efficiency boilers. Some systems are suitable for weather compensation, which allows return temperatures to fall into the condensing range for some periods of the heating season, and they may be best served by a mixture of condensing and non-condensing boilers.

The efficiency value that should be entered into accredited NCM tools to calculate the carbon dioxide emission rate is the effective heat generator seasonal efficiency. For boilers in new buildings, no heating efficiency credits can be gained and the effective heat generator seasonal efficiency is therefore the same as the heat generator seasonal efficiency.

Recommended minimum standards

To meet relevant energy efficiency requirements in the Building Regulations when installing boiler plant in new buildings:

a.   where a single boiler is used to meet the heat demand, its boiler seasonal efficiency (gross calorific value) calculated using Equation 2 should be not less than the value in Table 4

b.   for multiple-boiler systems, the boiler seasonal efficiency of each boiler should be not less than 82% (gross calorific value), as calculated using Equation 2; and the overall boiler seasonal efficiency of the multiple-boiler system, as defined by the three-step method and calculated using Equations 3.2 and 3.3, should be not less than the value in Table 4

c.   the relevant minimum controls package in Table 5 should be adopted.

Table 4 Recommended minimum heat generator seasonal efficiency for boiler systems in new buildings

Fuel type	System	Boiler seasonal efficiency (gross calorific value)
Natural gas	Single-boiler ≤ 2 MW output	91%
	Single-boiler > 2 MW output	86%
	Multiple-boiler	82% for any individual boiler 86% for overall multi-boiler system
LPG	Single-boiler ≤ 2 MW output	93%
	Single-boiler > 2 MW output	87%
	Multiple-boiler	82% for any individual boiler 87% for overall multi-boiler system
Oil	Single-boiler	84%
	Multiple-boiler	82% for any individual boiler 84% for overall multi-boiler system

Table 5 Recommended minimum controls package for new boilers and multiple-boiler systems

Boiler plant output	Package	Minimum controls
< 100 kW	A	a. Timing and temperature demand control, which should be zone specific where the building floor area is greater than 150 m². b. Weather compensation except where a constant temperature supply is required.
100 kW to 500 kW	B	a. Controls package A above. b. Optimum start/stop control with either night set-back or frost protection outside occupied periods. c. Two-stage high/low firing facility in boiler, or multiple boilers with sequence control to provide efficient part-load performance. Note: The heat loss from non-firing boiler modules should be limited by design or application. For boilers that do not have low standing losses, it may be necessary to install isolation valves or dampers.
> 500 kW individual boilers	C	a. Controls package A and controls package B. b. For gas-fired boilers and multi-stage oil-fired boilers, fully modulating burner controls.

2.6 Boilers in existing buildings

Background

Boiler efficiencies have improved markedly over recent years. A modern boiler meeting the minimum requirements of the Boiler Efficiency Directive has a boiler seasonal efficiency of approximately 78.5% (based on gross calorific value).

This guidance recognises that in many cases using condensing boiler technology in existing buildings would be either technically impractical (due to flueing constraints) or economically unviable. For this reason non-condensing boilers may be used provided that they meet the recommended minimum efficiency standards given in this section.

Replacement boilers

To meet relevant energy efficiency requirements in the Building Regulations when installing boiler plant in existing buildings:

a. the boiler seasonal efficiency of each boiler (in a single-boiler system or a multiple-boiler system with identical boilers) calculated using Equation 2 should be not less than the value in Table 6

b. for multiple-boiler systems using non-identical boilers, the overall boiler seasonal efficiency calculated using Equation 3.1 should be not less than the value in Table 6

c. the controls package in Table 7 should be adopted – i.e. zone control, demand control and time control

d. the effective boiler seasonal efficiency should be not less than the value in Table 6. To meet the standard, it may be necessary to adopt additional measures from Table 8 in order to gain heating efficiency credits (see below).

Table 6 Recommended minimum heat generator seasonal efficiency for boiler systems in existing buildings

Fuel type	Effective boiler seasonal efficiency (gross calorific value)	Boiler seasonal efficiency (gross calorific value)
Natural gas	84%	82%
LPG	85%	83%
Oil	86%	84%

Table 7 Recommended minimum controls package for replacement boilers in existing buildings

Minimum controls package	Suitable controls
a. Zone control	Zone control is required only for buildings where the floor area is greater than 150 m². As a minimum, on/off control (e.g. through an isolation valve for unoccupied zones) should be provided.
b. Demand control	Room thermostat which controls through a diverter valve with constant boiler flow water temperature. This method of control is not suitable for condensing boilers.
c. Time control	Time clock controls.

2.7 Heating efficiency credits for replacement boilers

Where the boiler seasonal efficiency is less than the minimum effective boiler seasonal efficiency for that type of boiler, additional measures will need to be adopted to achieve the minimum effective heat generator seasonal efficiency in Table 6.

Table 8 indicates the measures that may be adopted and the relevant heating efficiency credits that are applicable. It should be noted that the maximum number of heating efficiency credits that can be claimed is 4 percentage points.

Table 8 Heating efficiency credits for measures applicable to boiler replacement in existing buildings

Measure		Heating efficiency credits (% points)[13]	Comments
A	Boiler oversize ≤ 20%	2	Boiler oversize is defined as the amount by which the maximum boiler heat output exceeds the system heat output at design conditions, expressed as a percentage of that system heat output. For multiple-boiler systems the maximum boiler heat output is the sum of the maximum outputs of all the boilers in the system.
B	Multiple boilers	1	Where more than one boiler is used to meet the heat load.
C	Sequential control of multiple-boiler systems	1	Applies only to multiple-boiler/module arrangements. It is recommended that the most efficient boiler should act as the lead in a multiple-boiler system.
D	Monitoring and targeting	1	Means of identifying changes in operation or onset of faults. The credit can only be claimed if metering is included and a scheme for data collection is provided and available for inspection.
E	i. Thermostatic radiator valves (TRVs) alone. Would also apply to fanned convector systems	1	TRVs enable the building temperature to be controlled and therefore reduce waste of energy.
	ii. Weather (inside/outside temperature) compensation system using a mixing valve	1.5	Provides more accurate prediction of load and hence control.
	iii. Addition of TRV or temperature zone control to ii above to ensure full building temperature control	1	This credit is additional to Eii above.
F	i. A 'room' thermostat or sensor that controls boiler water temperature in relation to heat load	0.5	
	ii. Weather (inside/outside temperature) compensation system that is direct acting	2	Provides more accurate prediction of load and hence control.
	iii. Addition of TRV or temperature zone control to i or ii above to ensure full building temperature control	1	This credit is additional to Fi or Fii above. Note Fi and Fii are not used together.

13 The maximum that can be claimed is 4 points.

Table 8 Heating efficiency credits for measures applicable to boiler replacement in existing buildings *(continued)*

Measure		Heating efficiency credits (% points)[13]	Comments
G	i. Optimum start	1.5	A control system which starts plant operation at the latest time possible to achieve specified conditions at the start of the occupancy period.
	ii. Optimum stop	0.5	A control system which stops plant operation at the earliest possible time such that internal conditions will not deteriorate beyond preset limits by the end of the occupancy period.
	iii. Optimum start/stop	2	A control system which starts plant operation at the latest time possible to achieve specified conditions at the start of the occupancy period and stops plant operation at the earliest possible time such that internal conditions will not deteriorate beyond preset limits by the end of the occupancy period. Note that if optimum start/stop systems are installed, credits Gi and Gii cannot also be claimed.
H	Full zoned time control	1	Allowing each zone to operate independently in terms of start/stop time. Only applicable where operational conditions change in different zones. Does not include local temperature control.
I	Full building management system (BMS)	4	A full BMS linked to the heating plant will provide: sequential control of multiple boilers, full zoned time control and weather compensation where applicable; frost protection or night set-back; optimisation and monitoring and targeting. Note that if a full BMS is installed, no further heating efficiency credits can be claimed.
J	Decentralised heating system	1	Elimination of long pipe runs between buildings or through unheated areas in buildings in order to reduce excessive heat losses.

Example: Using heating efficiency credits to achieve the minimum effective heat generator seasonal efficiency for a boiler system in an existing building

An existing boiler is to be replaced with a gas boiler with a boiler seasonal efficiency of 82%, the minimum allowed by Table 6.

The boiler's effective boiler seasonal efficiency needs to be at least 84% according to Table 6, which means that 2 percentage points of heating efficiency credits are needed.

The following approach would achieve this:

a. restrict boiler oversizing to 15% (after a detailed assessment of load)

b. fit a room thermostat to control boiler water temperature in relation to heat load

c. use two equally sized boilers to meet the heat load in place of the existing single boiler

d. fit TRVs to control the temperature in areas other than where the room thermostat is fitted.

Table 9 below shows how credits would be awarded in this example.

Table 9 Example to illustrate allocation of heating efficiency credits for a replacement boiler in an existing building

Plant description	Heating efficiency credits (% points)
Boiler oversizing is less than 20%	2
System controlled by room thermostat which controls boiler water temperature	0.5
System uses TRVs to ensure full building temperature control	1
Multiple boilers	1
Total credits	**4.5**

Effective boiler seasonal efficiency

= boiler seasonal efficiency + maximum of 4 heating efficiency credits

= 82 + 4 = 86%

In this example the minimum effective boiler seasonal efficiency of 84% is exceeded by 2 percentage points.

2.8 Biomass boilers

Background

The method in Section 2.4 for calculating the seasonal efficiency of single and multiple boilers fired by gas, LPG and oil is not appropriate for biomass boilers.

For biomass boilers, requirements and test methods are covered by BS EN 12809:2001+A1:2004 *Residential independent boilers fired by solid fuel. Nominal heat output up to 50 kW. Requirements and test methods.*

Recommended minimum standards

To meet relevant energy efficiency requirements in the Building Regulations:

a. the efficiency of biomass boilers at their nominal load should be at least:

　i. 65% for independent gravity-fed boilers < 20.5 kW

　ii. 75% for independent automatic pellet/woodchip boilers

b. controls as for gas, LPG and oil boilers in Table 5 should be provided, where technically feasible.

Section 3: Heat pumps

3.1 Introduction

This section gives guidance on specifying heat pumps to provide space heating and domestic hot water in new and existing buildings to meet relevant energy efficiency requirements in the Building Regulations.

The heat pumps covered in this section take heat energy from a low temperature source and upgrade it to a higher temperature at which it can be usefully employed for heating.

The guidance covers measures, such as additional controls, that can be used to gain heating efficiency credits to improve the coefficient of performance of heat pumps.

For guidance on reverse cycle heat pumps that also provide cooling, see Section 9 of this guide.

3.2 Scope of guidance

The guidance in this section applies to the commercial heat pump systems identified in Table 10, which categorises the different types of heat pump according to:

- the source of the heat
- the medium by which it is delivered, and
- the technology.

Table 10 Heat pump types and associated test standards

Heat pump type	Technology	Sub-technology	Test standard
Electrically-driven warm air	Ground-to-air	Single package + variable refrigerant flow warm air systems	ISO 13256-1[14]
		Energy transfer systems (matching heating/cooling demands in buildings)	
	Water-to-air	Single package + variable refrigerant flow warm air systems	BS EN 14511-3[15]
		Energy transfer systems (matching heating/cooling demands in buildings)	
	Air-to-air	Single package	BS EN 14511-3
		Split system	
		Multi-split system	
		Variable refrigerant flow systems	
Electrically-driven warm water	Ground-to-water	Single package + variable refrigerant flow warm air systems	ISO 13256-2[16]
		Split package	
	Water-to-water	Single package + variable refrigerant flow warm air systems	BS EN 14511-3
		Split package	
	Air-to-water	Single package	BS EN 14511-3
		Split package + variable refrigerant flow warm air systems	
Gas-engine-driven	Available as variable refrigerant flow warm air systems		Generally to BS EN 14511-3

14   ISO 13256-1 *Water-source heat pumps. Testing and rating for performance. Part 1: Water-to-air and brine-to-air heat pumps.*
15   BS EN 14511-3:2013 *Air conditioners, liquid chilling packages and heat pumps with electrically driven compressors for space heating and cooling. Test methods.*
16   ISO 13256-2 *Water-source heat pumps. Testing and rating for performance. Part 2: Water-to-water and brine-to-water heat pumps.*

3.3 Key terms

Coefficient of performance (COP) is a measure of the efficiency of a heat pump at specified source and sink temperatures, but may not accurately represent installed performance:

Heating COP = heat output / power input   **Equation 4**

% COP (COP × 100) is the heat generator efficiency.

Effective % COP is the % COP with heating efficiency credits.

The COP of a heat pump should be determined in accordance with the appropriate test standard identified in Table 10. The input power items to be included in the calculation are defined in the standard.

Seasonal coefficient of performance (SCOP) is the overall coefficient of performance of the unit for the designated heating season. It makes general assumptions about the amount of auxiliary heating needed to top up the space and water heating available from the heat pump.

SCOP is measured in accordance with the procedures in BS EN 14825:2013 *Air conditioners, liquid chilling packages and heat pumps with electrically driven compressors for space heating and cooling. Testing and rating at part load conditions and calculation of seasonal performance.*

The National Calculation Methodology for calculating carbon dioxide emission rates from buildings uses SCOP.

Seasonal performance factor (SPF) is another measure of the operating performance of an electric heat pump over the season. It is the ratio of the heat delivered to the total electrical energy supplied over the season, but there are up to seven different ways to draw the system boundaries. For example, SPF_{H2} excludes auxiliary resistance heating while SPF_{H4} includes it – making a large difference.

SAP 2012 calculations (for dwellings) use SPF – either measured values for products listed in the Product Characteristics Database, or the default values in Table 4a for products not listed there.

The Microgeneration Certification Scheme installation standard, MIS 3005, uses SPF to calculate system performance (although the heat pump product standard, MCS 007, currently specifies a minimum COP).

Seasonal primary energy efficiency ratio (SPEER) is an emerging rating figure reflecting the use of primary energy for all types of heat pump, fossil fuel boiler and gas-driven cogeneration technologies, as well as hybrid systems where solar heating or a heat pump is backed up with electric heating or a fossil fuel boiler.

Energy labelling with the SPEER will be mandatory from 2015 under the Energy Labelling Directive. Testing and rating will be in accordance with BS EN 14825, as for SCOP.

3.4 Heat pumps in new and existing buildings

At the time of preparation of this guide, European Commission Regulation No 206/2012 sets standards only for the SCOP of electrically-driven air-to-air heat pumps with an output ≤ 12 kW. There are currently no European test standards for part-load testing of air-to-air heat pumps with an output > 12 kW or for other types of heat pump[17], and so the performance of these must be specified using COP obtained at the heating system rating conditions.

---

17   Requirements for heat pumps delivering water with an output up to 400 kW are expected to come into force in August 2015.

The current recommendations in this guide are that heat pumps in new and existing buildings should:

a. if air-to-air with an output ≤ 12 kW, have at least a SCOP 'D' rating for the median temperature range in BS EN 14825

b. or else have a COP which is not less than the value in Table 11

c. feature as a minimum the controls package in Table 12.

Table 11 Recommended minimum COP for heat pumps in new and existing buildings

Heat pump type	Minimum COP at the rating conditions[18]
All types (except air-to-air with output ≤ 12 kW, absorption and gas-engine) for space heating	2.5
All types (except absorption and gas-engine) for domestic hot water heating	2.0
Absorption	0.5
Gas-engine	1.0

For non-residential buildings, the heat pump system can be sized to meet either the full heating and hot water demand or part of it. Economically viable installations provide at least 50% of the heating and hot water demand for the building.

Table 12 Recommended minimum controls package for heat pump systems in new and existing buildings

Heat source/sink	Technology		Minimum controls package
All types	All technologies	A	a. On/off zone control. If the unit serves a single zone, and for buildings with a floor area of 150 m² or less, the minimum requirement is achieved by default. b. Time control.

Air-to-air	Single package
	
	Split system
	
	Multi-split system
	
	Variable refrigerant flow system
		B	a. Controls package A above.
			b. Heat pump unit controls for:
			  i. control of room air temperature (if not provided externally)
			  ii. control of outdoor fan operation
			  iii. defrost control of external airside heat exchanger
			  iv. control for secondary heating (if fitted).
			c. External room thermostat (if not provided in the heat pump unit) to regulate the space temperature and interlocked with the heat pump unit operation.

18 Rating conditions are standardised conditions for determining performance specified in BS EN 14511:2013 *Air conditioners, liquid chilling packages and heat pumps with electrically driven compressors for space heating and cooling.*

Table 12 Recommended minimum controls package for heat pump systems in new and existing buildings (continued)

Heat source/sink	Technology		Minimum controls package
Water-to-air Ground-to-air	Single package energy transfer systems (matching heating/ cooling demand in buildings)	D	a. Controls package A above. b. Heat pump unit controls for: i. control of room air temperature (if not provided externally) ii. control of outdoor fan operation for cooling tower or dry cooler (energy transfer systems) iii. control for secondary heating (if fitted) on air-to-air systems iv. control of external water pump operation. c. External room thermostat (if not provided in the heat pump unit) to regulate the space temperature and interlocked with the heat pump unit operation.
Air-to-water Water-to-water Ground-to-water	Single package Split package	E	a. Controls package A above. b. Heat pump unit controls for: i. control of water pump operation (internal and external as appropriate) ii. control of water temperature for the distribution system iii. control of outdoor fan operation for air-to-water units iv. defrost control of external airside heat exchanger for air-to-water systems. c. External room thermostat (if not provided in the heat pump unit) to regulate the space temperature and interlocked with the heat pump unit operation.
Gas-engine-driven heat pumps are currently available only as variable refrigerant flow warm air systems	Multi-split Variable refrigerant flow	F	a. Controls package A above. b. Heat pump unit controls for: i. control of room air temperature (if not provided externally) ii. control of outdoor fan operation iii. defrost control of external airside heat exchanger iv. control for secondary heating (if fitted). c. External room thermostat (if not provided in the heat pump unit) to regulate the space temperature and interlocked with the heat pump unit operation.

3.5 Heating efficiency credits for heat pump systems in existing buildings

Heating efficiency credits can be gained for heat pump systems installed in existing buildings by adopting the additional measures in Table 13. These credits are added to the % COP to produce the effective % COP.

Table 13 Heating efficiency credits for additional measures applicable to heat pump systems in existing buildings

Measure	Heating efficiency credits (% points)	Comments
< 20% oversizing	2	The amount by which the maximum heat pump output exceeds the system heat output at design conditions, expressed as a percentage of that system heat output.
Optimum stop	2	A control system which stops plant operation at the earliest possible time such that internal conditions will not deteriorate beyond preset limits by the end of the occupancy period.
Full zone control	2	Allows each zone to operate independently in terms of start/stop time. Only appropriate where operational conditions change in different zones.
Monitoring and targeting	2	Means of identifying changes in operation or onset of faults.

Example: Using heating efficiency credits to achieve the recommended standard for effective % COP for a heat pump installation

A proposed system has an air-to-water, electrically-driven heat pump supplying heat to an underfloor heating system. The COP of the heat pump tested to BS EN 14511 is 2.46, which is below the minimum standard recommended by Table 11 for space heating.

The minimum controls package recommended by Table 12 is package E, comprising:

a. zone control and time control

b. heat pump unit controls for:

   i.   control of outdoor fan operation for cooling tower or dry cooler (energy transfer systems)

   ii. control of external water pump operation and water temperature for the distribution system

c. room thermostat to regulate the space temperature and interlocked with the heat pump unit operation.

Table 14 shows the heating efficiency credits that can be gained by adding optimum stop control and full zone control.

Effective % COP = % COP + heating efficiency credits = 246 + 4 = 250%

The effective COP is therefore 2.50, which meets the minimum required by Table 11.

Table 14 Example to illustrate the allocation of heating efficiency credits to a new heat pump system in an existing building

Measure	Heating efficiency credits (% points)
Measures specified in controls package A	0 (as this is the minimum standard)
Measures specified in controls package E	0 (as this is the minimum standard)
Optimum stop	2
Full zone control	2
Total credits	4

3.6 Supplementary information

Heat source/sink	Technology	Comments
Air-to-air	Single package	Units may be ducted on one or other of the supply and return air sides or ducted on both sides. Ducting needs to be designed to take into account the maximum specific fan power allowable (see Section 10 of this guide) and to maintain the minimum allowable coefficient of performance.
	Split Multi-split Variable refrigerant flow Gas-engine-driven	A split system will comprise a single outdoor unit and a single indoor unit as a package. Multi-split and variable refrigerant flow systems will comprise a single outdoor unit and two or more indoor units as a package. Several packages may be used to satisfy the requirements of the building. In order for efficiencies to be maintained, all connecting pipework should be installed in accordance with manufacturers' recommendations (diameter, length, insulation and riser height). Any ducting should be designed to take into account the maximum specific fan power allowable and to maintain the minimum allowable coefficient of performance.
Water-to-air Ground-to-air	Single package Energy transfer	Energy transfer systems generally consist of multiple water-source heat pumps connected in parallel to a common closed water loop. They are installed to offset the simultaneous heating and cooling demand in a building due to the different loads present on the aspects of the building. Water circulation pumps for the closed loop should be taken into consideration along with the fan power required for the cooling tower or dry cooler or energy for water pumps for the ground loop if this method is utilised for heat injection and rejection. Any ducting should be designed to take into account the maximum specific fan power allowable and to maintain the minimum allowable coefficient of performance.
Air-to-water Water-to-ground Water-to-water	Single package Split package	Water circulation pumps for the delivery of heated water to the building along with the energy of water pumps used for the heat source (water or ground) should be considered in the calculation. Any ducting should be designed to take into account the maximum specific fan power allowable and to maintain the minimum allowable coefficient of performance.

Additional guidance on design criteria for heating systems with integrated heat pumps is given in BS EN 15450:2007 *Heating systems in buildings. Design of heat pump heating systems.*

Section 4: Gas and oil-fired warm air heaters

4.1 Introduction

This section gives guidance on specifying gas and oil-fired warm air heaters for space heating in new and existing buildings to meet relevant energy efficiency requirements in the Building Regulations. It includes guidance on measures, such as additional controls, that can be used to gain heating efficiency credits to improve the heat generator seasonal efficiency.

4.2 Scope of guidance

The guidance in this section covers the warm air heaters listed in Table 15. The guidance also covers indirect gas or oil-fired heat exchangers (as used in large ducted systems for office blocks, shopping and leisure complexes, etc.) to provide heating and fresh or conditioned air. Warm air central heating systems are not within the scope of this section but are covered in the relevant heat generator section and Section 10 *Air distribution*.

Table 15 Warm air heaters and test methods

Type of warm air heater		Product standard
Type 1	Gas-fired forced convection without a fan to assist transportation of combustion air and/or combustion products	BS EN 621:2009[19]
Type 2	Gas-fired forced convection incorporating a fan to assist transportation of combustion air and/or combustion products	BS EN 1020:2009[20]
Type 3	Direct gas-fired forced convection	BS EN 525:2009[21]
Type 4	Oil-fired forced convection	BS EN 13842:2004[22]

4.3 Key terms

Heat generator seasonal efficiency of air heaters, since they operate under the same conditions at all times, is equivalent to their measured steady state thermal efficiency (net calorific value), which can be obtained from the heater manufacturer's data and converted to efficiency (gross calorific value) using the conversion factors in SAP 2012 Table E4.

For indirect-fired heaters, data values for heat output and net heat input are measured using the efficiency test methods described in BS EN 1020, BS EN 621 or BS EN 13842 as appropriate.

For direct-fired heaters, the efficiency should be calculated using the method described in BS EN 525.

19 BS EN 621:2009 Non-domestic gas-fired forced convection air heaters for space heating not exceeding a net heat input of 300 kW, without a fan to assist transportation of combustion air and/or combustion products.
20 BS EN 1020:2009 Non-domestic forced convection gas-fired air heaters for space heating not exceeding a net heat input of 300 kW, incorporating a fan to assist transportation of combustion air or combustion products.
21 BS EN 525:2009 Non-domestic direct gas-fired forced convection air heaters for space heating not exceeding a net heat input of 300 kW.
22 BS EN 13842:2004 Oil-fired convection air heaters. Stationary and transportable for space heating.

The calculation of the thermal efficiency (net) should:

- take account of the heater and the exhaust chimney within the building envelope
- exclude fans.

Effective heat generator seasonal efficiency is the heat generator seasonal efficiency with added heating efficiency credits (see below). It is the value entered into NCM tools such as SBEM to calculate the building carbon dioxide emission rate (BER).

4.4 Warm air heaters in new and existing buildings

Warm air systems in new and existing buildings should have:

a. an effective heat generator seasonal efficiency which is no worse than in Table 16

b. a controls package featuring, as a minimum, time control, space temperature control and, where appropriate for buildings with a floor area greater than 150 m², zone control.

Table 16 Recommended minimum effective heat generator seasonal efficiency

Warm air heater type (see Table 15)	Effective heat generator seasonal efficiency (net calorific value)
Types 1, 2 natural gas	91%
Types 1, 2 LPG	91%
Type 3*	100%
Type 4	91%

* For Type 3 air heaters, 100% of the net heat input is delivered to the space. Specific ventilation requirements as defined in BS EN 525 should be met.

4.5 Heating efficiency credits for warm air heaters in new and existing buildings

Heating efficiency credits can be gained by adopting the additional measures listed in Table 17.

Table 17 Heating efficiency credits for additional measures applicable to warm air heaters

Measure	Heating efficiency credits (% points)	Comments
Optimum stop	1	A control system which stops plant operation at the earliest possible time such that internal conditions will not deteriorate beyond preset limits by the end of the occupancy period.
Hi/Lo burners	2	Two-stage burners which enable two distinct firing rates.
Modulating burners	3	Burner controls which allow continuous adjustment of the firing rate.

Destratification fans and air-induction schemes

It is recognised that destratification fans and air-induction schemes may improve the efficiency of a warm air system and significantly reduce the carbon emissions associated with the heating system. The benefits of these measures are already taken into account by the NCM so no heating efficiency credits can be gained by using them. Note that warm air systems with air induction schemes or destratification fans should not be confused with central heating systems that have air distribution.

Example: Using heating efficiency credits to exceed the minimum effective heat generator seasonal efficiency for a warm air heater

A proposed building has a gas-fired forced-convection warm air heater without a fan to assist transportation of combustion air or combustion products. When tested to BS EN 621:2009 the thermal efficiency (net calorific value) is found to be 91%, which meets the minimum effective heat generating efficiency recommended for this type of system in Table 16.

The minimum controls package specified in paragraph 4.4b comprises zone, space temperature and time controls. Table 18 shows how credits are awarded by adding optimum stop control, modulating burners and destratification fans.

Table 18 Example to illustrate the allocation of heating efficiency credits to a warm air heater system	
Measure	**Heating efficiency credits** (% points)
Zone, space and temperature controls	0 (as this is the minimum standard)
Modulating burners	3
Optimum stop	1
Destratification fans	0 (as the benefits are already recognised by the NCM)
Total credits	**4**

Effective heat generator seasonal efficiency = net thermal efficiency + heating efficiency credits

= 91 + 4 = 95%

The effective heat generator seasonal efficiency is therefore 95%, exceeding the minimum standard by 4 percentage points. The value that should be entered into the accredited NCM tool to calculate the carbon dioxide emission rate is 95%.

Section 5: Gas and oil-fired radiant heaters

5.1 Introduction

This section gives guidance on specifying radiant heaters for space heating in new and existing buildings to meet relevant energy efficiency requirements in the Building Regulations. It includes guidance on measures, such as additional controls, that can be used to gain heating efficiency credits to improve the heat generator seasonal efficiency.

5.2 Scope of guidance

The guidance in this section covers the types of radiant heater listed in Table 19.

Table 19 Types of radiant heater and associated product standards

Radiant heater type	Product standard
Luminous radiant heater	BS EN 419-1:2009[23]
Non-luminous radiant heater	BS EN 416-1:2009[24]
Multi-burner radiant heater	BS EN 777 series[25]
Oil-fired radiant heater	N/A

5.3 Key terms

Radiant heater seasonal efficiency (heat generator seasonal efficiency) is equivalent to thermal efficiency (net calorific value).

For flued appliances, the manufacturer of the radiant heater should declare a thermal efficiency measured to the test standards BS EN 1020[26] or BS EN 13842[27] as applicable.

The calculation of the thermal efficiency (net calorific value) should:

a. take account of the radiant heater and associated flue pipe/tailpipe within the building envelope

b. exclude fans.

---

23   BS EN 419-1:2009 *Non-domestic gas-fired overhead luminous radiant heaters. Safety.*
24   BS EN 416-1:2009 *Single-burner gas-fired overhead radiant tube heaters. Safety.*
25   BS EN 777-1:2009 *Multi-burner gas-fired overhead radiant tube heater systems for non-domestic use. System D. Safety.*
     BS EN 777-2:2009 *Multi-burner gas-fired overhead radiant tube heater systems for non-domestic use. System E. Safety.*
     BS EN 777-3:2009 *Multi-burner gas-fired overhead radiant tube heater systems for non-domestic use. System F. Safety.*
     BS EN 777-4:2009 *Multi-burner gas-fired overhead radiant tube heater systems for non-domestic use. System H. Safety.*
26   BS EN 1020:2009 *Non-domestic forced convection gas-fired air heaters for space heating not exceeding a net heat input of 300 kW, incorporating a fan to assist transportation of combustion air or combustion products.*
27   BS EN 13842:2004 *Oil-fired convection air heaters. Stationary and transportable for space heating.*

5.4 Radiant heaters

Radiant heaters in new and existing buildings should have:

a. an effective heat generator seasonal efficiency not worse than in Table 20

b. a controls package consisting of, as a minimum, time control and space temperature control with black bulb sensors.

Table 20 Recommended minimum performance standards for radiant heaters

Appliance type	Effective heat generator seasonal efficiency	
	Thermal	Radiant
Luminous radiant heater – unflued	86%	55%
Non-luminous radiant heater – unflued	86%	55%
Non-luminous radiant heater – flued	86%	55%
Multi-burner radiant heater	91%	N/A

5.5 Heating efficiency credits for radiant heaters in existing buildings

Heating efficiency credits can be gained by adopting the additional measures listed in Table 21. They are added to the heat generator seasonal efficiency (the thermal efficiency – net calorific value) to give the effective heat generator seasonal efficiency.

Table 21 Heating efficiency credits for additional measures applicable to radiant heaters

Measure		Heating efficiency credits (% points)	Comments
Controls (additional to the minimum package)	Optimum stop	1	A control system which stops plant operation at the earliest possible time such that internal conditions will not deteriorate beyond preset limits by the end of the occupancy period.
	Optimum start	0.5	A control system which starts plant operation at the latest possible time such that internal conditions will be up to required limits at the start of the occupancy period.
	Zone control	1	A control system in which each zone operates independently in terms of start/stop time. It is only appropriate where operational conditions change in different zones.

Example: Using heating efficiency credits to achieve the minimum effective heat generator seasonal efficiency for a radiant heater system

A proposed building will have a flued non-luminous radiant heater system with a thermal efficiency (heat generator seasonal efficiency) of 84%. A black bulb sensor and an optimiser will be fitted.

The heating efficiency credits associated with these measures are added to the appliance thermal efficiency to obtain the effective heat generator seasonal efficiency.

Table 22 shows how credits are awarded for this example.

Table 22 Example to illustrate the allocation of heating efficiency credits to a radiant heater system	
Measure	**Heating efficiency credits** (% points)
Black bulb sensor	0 (as minimum requirement)
Optimum stop	1
Zone control	1
Total credits	**2**

Effective heat generator seasonal efficiency = thermal efficiency + heating efficiency credits

= 84 + 2 = 86%

In this example, the application of additional measures to gain heating efficiency credits has brought the radiant heater's effective heat generator seasonal efficiency up to the minimum recommended value.

Section 6: Combined heat and power and community heating

6.1 Introduction

This section gives guidance on specifying combined heat and power (CHP) systems for space heating, hot water and chilled water (via absorption chillers) in new and existing buildings to meet relevant energy efficiency requirements in the Building Regulations. Guidance on the design of community heating systems can be found in Section 6 of the *Domestic Building Services Compliance Guide*.

CHP units are normally used in conjunction with boilers. The majority of the annual heat demand is usually provided by the CHP plant, while the boilers are used to meet peak demand and in periods when the CHP unit is not operating (for example at night or when undergoing maintenance).

CHP units may on a relatively small scale supply single buildings, or on a larger scale supply a number of buildings through a community heating system. The most common fuel is natural gas, which can be used in spark-ignition gas engines, micro-turbines, or gas turbines in open cycle or combined cycle.

6.2 Scope of guidance

The guidance in this section covers CHP systems with a total power capacity less than 5 MWe used in commercial applications. The CHP units may or may not supply community heating.

Guidance on community heating systems with micro-CHP (having a total power capacity less than 5 kWe) and other heat generators is available in the *Domestic Building Services Compliance Guide*.

6.3 Key terms

Combined heat and power (CHP) means the simultaneous generation of heat and power in a single process. The power output is usually electricity, but may include mechanical power. Heat outputs can include steam, hot water or hot air for process heating, space heating or absorption cooling.

Combined Heat and Power Quality Assurance (CHPQA) is a scheme[28] under which registration and certification of CHP systems is carried out according to defined quality criteria.

CHPQA quality index is an indicator of the energy efficiency and environmental performance of a CHP scheme relative to generation of the same amounts of heat and power by alternative means.

Power efficiency is the total annual power output divided by the total annual fuel input of a CHP unit.

---

28   Further information about the CHPQA programme is available at www.chpqa.com.

6.4 CHP in new and existing buildings

CHP plant in new and existing buildings should have:

a.   a minimum CHPQA quality index (QI) of 105 and power efficiency greater than 20%, both under annual operation

b.   a control system that, as a minimum, ensures that the CHP unit operates as the lead heat generator

c.   metering to measure hours run, electricity generated and fuel supplied to the CHP unit.

The CHP plant should be sized to supply not less than 45% of the annual total heating demand (i.e. space heating, domestic hot water heating and process heating) unless there are overriding practical or economic constraints.

Calculating the carbon dioxide emissions from a CHP heating system

CHP may be used as a main or supplementary heat source in community heating systems. To calculate the carbon dioxide emission rate for a new building for the purposes of showing compliance with the Building Regulations, the following data will need to be entered into an accredited NCM tool such as SBEM:

a.   the proportion (P %) of the annual heat demand (H MWh) to be supplied by the CHP plant (H×P). This is needed as the CHP unit is normally sized below the peak heat demand of the building and will also be out of service for maintenance purposes

b.   the overall efficiency ratio of the CHP plant (E) as defined by Equation 5 and taking account of part-load operation and all heat rejection predicted by an operating model:

E = (annual useful heat supplied + annual electricity generated net of parasitic electricity use)/annual energy of the fuel supplied (in gross calorific value terms)   **Equation 5**

c.   the heat to power ratio of the CHP plant (R), calculated for the annual operation according to Equation 6:

R = annual useful heat supplied/annual electricity generated net of parasitic electricity use
                                                                                                              Equation 6

The carbon dioxide emitted in kg/year for the heat supplied by a gas-fired CHP plant is then:

$$\left[\left(\frac{H \times P}{E} + \frac{H \times P}{R \times E} \right) \times 216 \right] - \left[\frac{H \times P}{R} \times 519 \right]$$

where 216 and 519 are the assumed carbon dioxide emission factors in g/kWh for mains gas and grid-displaced electricity respectively.   **Equation 7**

The carbon dioxide emitted for the balance of heat supplied by the boilers is then calculated by the NCM tool as for a boiler only system.

6.5 Supplementary information

Community heating systems may include other low and zero carbon sources of energy such as biomass heating. Emission factors should be determined based on the particular details of the scheme, but should take account of the annual average performance of the whole system – that is, of the distribution circuits and all the heat generating plant, including any CHP and any waste heat recovery or heat dumping. The calculation of the building carbon dioxide emission rate should be carried out by a suitably qualified person, who should explain how the emission factors were derived.

The design of the community heating connection and the building's heating control system should take account of the requirements of the community heating organisation with respect to maintaining low return temperatures at part-load and limiting the maximum flow rate to be supplied by the community heating system to the agreed level. A heat meter should be installed to measure the heat energy supplied and to monitor the maximum heat demand, the maximum community heating flow rate and the return temperatures into the community heating network.

Further guidance can be found in the following documents:

* Carbon Trust GPG 234 *Community heating and CHP*

* CIBSE AM12 *Small-scale CHP for buildings*

* HVCA TR/30 *Guide to good practice – Heat pumps.*

Section 7: Direct electric space heating

7.1 Introduction

This section gives guidance on specifying direct electric heaters for space heating in new and existing buildings. It addresses the relevant electric heater types and the minimum provision of controls.

7.2 Scope of guidance

The guidance given in this section covers the following types of electric heating systems, which may be used to provide primary or secondary space heating:

- electric boilers

- electric warm air systems

- electric panel heaters

- electric storage systems, including integrated storage/direct systems

- electric fan heaters and fan convector heaters

- electric radiant heaters, including quartz and ceramic types.

The guidance does not cover electric heat pumps or portable electric heating devices.

7.3 Electric space heating in new and existing buildings

It is assumed that electric heating devices convert electricity to heat within a building with an efficiency of 100%. A minimum heat generator seasonal efficiency is therefore not specified.

Electric space heating systems in new and existing buildings should meet the minimum standards for:

a. controls for electric boilers in Table 23

b. controls for electric heating systems other than boilers in Table 24.

Table 23 Recommended minimum controls for electric boiler systems

Type of control	Standard	Comments
Boiler temperature control	a. Boiler fitted with a flow temperature control and capable of modulating the power input to the primary water depending on space heating conditions.	
Zoning	b. For buildings with a total usable floor area greater than 150 m², at least two space heating zones with independent time and temperature controls using either: i. multiple heating zone programmers, or ii. a single multi-channel programmer.	
Temperature control of space heating	c. Separate temperature control of zones within the building using either: i. room thermostats or programmable room thermostats in all zones, or ii. a room thermostat or programmable room thermostat in the main zone and individual radiator controls such as thermostatic radiator valves (TRVs) on all radiators in the other zones, or iii. a combination of (i) and (ii) above.	
Time control of space and water heating	d. Provide using: i. a full programmer with separate time control for each circuit, or ii. separate timers for each circuit, or iii. programmable room thermostats for the heating circuits, with separate time control for all the circuits.	

Note: An acceptable alternative to the above controls is any boiler management control system that meets the specified zoning, timing and temperature requirements.

Table 24 Recommended minimum controls for primary and secondary electric heating systems other than electric boilers

Type of electric heating system	Type of control	Standard	Comments
Warm air	Time and temperature control, either integral to the heater or external	a. A time switch/programmer and room thermostat, or b. a programmable room thermostat.	
	Zone control	c. For buildings with a total usable floor area greater than 150 m², at least two space heating circuits with independent timing and temperature controls using either: i. multiple heating zone programmers, or ii. a single multi-channel programmer.	
Radiant heaters	Zone or occupancy control	a. Connection to a passive infra-red detector.	Electric radiant heaters can provide zone heating or be used for a full heating scheme. Common electric radiant heaters include the quartz and ceramic types.
Panel/skirting heaters	Local time and temperature control	a. Time control provided by: i. a programmable time switch integrated into the appliance, or ii. a separate time switch. b. Individual temperature control provided by: i. integral thermostats, or ii. separate room thermostats.	Panel heater systems provide instantaneous heat.
Storage heaters	Charge control	a. Automatic control of input charge (based on an ability to detect the internal temperature and adjust the charging of the heater accordingly).	
	Temperature control	b. Manual controls for adjusting the rate of heat release from the appliance, such as adjustable damper or some other thermostatically-controlled means.	
Fan/fan convector heaters	Local fan control	a. A switch integrated into the appliance, or b. a separate remote switch.	
	Individual temperature control	c. Integral switches, or d. separate remote switching.	

Section 8: Domestic hot water

8.1 Introduction

This section gives guidance on specifying domestic hot water (DHW) systems for new and existing buildings to meet relevant energy efficiency requirements in the Building Regulations. It includes guidance on measures, such as additional controls, that can be used to gain heating efficiency credits to improve the heat generator seasonal efficiency.

Note: Water quality can have a major impact on system efficiency. It is important that designers take appropriate measures to ensure that the system water is of good quality.

As well as the Building Regulations, other regulations apply to the provision of domestic hot water. Energy-saving measures should not compromise the safety of people or the ability of the system to achieve approved regimes for the control of legionella.

Domestic hot water systems are referred to as hot water service systems in SBEM.

8.2 Scope of guidance

The guidance in this section covers the conventional direct and indirect gas-fired, oil-fired and electrically-heated domestic hot water systems shown in Table 25.

The recommended minimum standards set out in this section apply only to dedicated water heaters. Central heating boilers which provide space heating and domestic hot water should meet the minimum standards in Section 2; and heat pumps which provide domestic hot water should meet the minimum standards in Section 3.

The guidance in this section applies to back-up gas and electric systems used with solar thermal hot water systems, but not to solar thermal systems themselves. For solar systems with a cylinder capacity of less than 440 litres or collector surface area less than 20 m², consult the DCLG *Domestic Building Services Compliance Guide*, or for larger systems, the CIBSE *Solar heating design and installation guide*.

Table 25 Types of hot water system

Direct-fired circulator: natural gas and LPG	A system in which the water is supplied to the draw-off points from a hot water vessel in which water is heated by combustion gases from a primary energy source. The unit has no storage volume as water is stored in a supplementary storage vessel.
Direct-fired storage: natural gas, LPG and oil	A system in which the water is supplied to the draw-off points from an integral hot water vessel in which water is heated by combustion gases from a primary energy source.
Direct-fired continuous flow: natural gas and LPG	A system in which the water is supplied to the draw-off points from a device in which cold water is heated by combustion gases from a primary energy source as it flows through the water heater. The water heater is situated close to the draw-off points. The unit has no storage volume as water is instantaneously heated as it flows through the device.
Indirect-fired circulator: natural gas, LPG and oil	A system in which the water is supplied to the draw-off points from a device in which water is heated by means of an element through which the heating medium is circulated in such a manner that it does not mix with the hot water supply. In practice the heat source is likely to be a boiler dedicated to the supply of domestic hot water.
Instantaneous electrically-heated	A system in which the water is supplied to the draw-off points from a device in which cold water is heated by an electric element or elements as it flows through the water heater. The water heater is situated close to the draw-off points. The unit has no storage volume as water is instantaneously heated as it flows through the device.
Point-of-use electrically-heated	A system in which the water is supplied to the draw-off points from a device in which water is heated by an electric element or elements immersed in the stored water. The water heater is situated close to the draw-off points and should have a storage capacity no greater than 100 litres.
Local electrically-heated	A system in which the water is supplied to the draw-off points from a device in which water is heated by an electric element or elements immersed in the stored water. The water heater is situated in the locality of the draw-off points and should have a storage capacity of between 100 and 300 litres. Bulk heating of the water heater should be with off-peak electricity.
Centralised electrically-heated	A system in which the water is supplied to the draw-off points from a device in which water is heated by an electric element or elements immersed in the stored water. The water heater is situated centrally with a distribution system to supply water to the draw off-points and should have a capacity greater than 300 litres. Bulk heating of the water heater should be with off-peak electricity.

8.3 Key terms

The heat generator seasonal efficiency is defined for each system type in Table 26.

The effective heat generator seasonal efficiency is the heat generator seasonal efficiency plus heating efficiency credits gained by adopting additional measures from Table 31.

Table 26 Definition of heat generator seasonal efficiency for DHW systems

DHW system type	Heat generator seasonal efficiency	Comments on calculation[1]
Direct-fired circulator: natural gas and LPG	Equals the thermal efficiency of the heater (gross calorific value) when tested to BS EN 15502-2-1:2012[29],[2]	**Exclude:** a. secondary pipework b. fans and pumps c. diverter valves, solenoids, actuators d. supplementary storage vessels.
Direct-fired storage: natural gas, LPG and oil	Equals the thermal efficiency of the heater (gross calorific value) when tested using the procedures in BS EN 89:2000[30],[2]	**Include** the water heater and insulation of the integral storage vessel only.
Direct-fired continuous flow: natural gas and LPG	Equals the thermal efficiency of the heater (gross calorific value) when tested to BS EN 26:1998[31].	**Exclude:** a. secondary pipework b. fans and pumps c. diverter valves, solenoids, actuators d. supplementary storage vessels.
Indirect-fired circulator: natural gas, LPG and oil	Calculate using Equations 2, 3.1, or 3.2 and 3.3 (as appropriate) in Section 2. Use Equation 2 $(0.81\eta_{30\%} + 0.19\eta_{100\%})$ to calculate boiler seasonal efficiency if primary return temperature $\leq 55°C$. Use boiler full load efficiency $(1.0\eta_{100\%})$ at 80/60°C flow/return temperatures if primary return temperature $> 55°C$. If boiler seasonal efficiency values are obtained as net values the factors in SAP 2012 Table E4 should be used to convert to gross values.	**Include** the heat generator only.
Electrically-heated	These are assumed 100% thermally efficient in terms of conversion to heat within the building.	

Notes

[1] For hot water systems in new buildings, standing losses are calculated in the accredited NCM tool.

[2] Where efficiency data is not readily available, efficiencies can be calculated using manufacturers' recovery rates and the following equations:

Gross thermal efficiency = heater output / gross input **Equation 8**

Heater output = recovery rate of heater in litres/second × specific heat capacity of water × temperature rise of water **Equation 9**

29   BS EN 15502-2-1:2012 *Specific standard for type C appliances and type B2, B3 and B5 appliances of a nominal heat input not exceeding 1000 kW.*

30   BS EN 89:2000 *Gas fired water heaters for the production of domestic hot water. Direct-fired storage water heaters, Section 8.2, Maintenance consumption.*

31   BS EN 26:1998 *Gas fired instantaneous water heaters for the production of domestic hot water, fitted with atmospheric burners.*

8.4 Domestic hot water systems in new and existing buildings

Domestic hot water systems in new and existing buildings should meet the recommended minimum standards for:

a. heat losses from DHW storage vessels in Table 27, or maintenance consumption values in BS EN 89:2000

b. heat generator efficiency (gross calorific value) in Table 28

c. controls in Tables 29 and 30.

Table 27 Recommended maximum heat losses from DHW storage vessels

Nominal volume (litres)	Heat loss (kWh/24h)	Nominal volume (litres)	Heat loss (kWh/24h)
200	2.1	900	4.5
300	2.6	1000	4.7
400	3.1	1100	4.8
500	3.5	1200	4.9
600	3.8	1300	5.0
700	4.1	1500	5.1
800	4.3	2000	5.2

Notes

[1] For guidance on maximum heat losses from DHW storage vessels with a storage volume less than 200 litres, see BS EN 15450:2007[32].

[2] The heat loss from electrically-heated cylinders (volume V litres) should not exceed $1.28 \times (0.2 + 0.051V^{2/3})$ if point-of-use or $1.28 \times (0.051V^{2/3})$ if local.

---

32   BS EN 15450:2007 *Heating systems in buildings. Design of heat pump heating systems.*

Table 28 Recommended minimum thermal efficiencies for domestic hot water systems

DHW system type	Fuel type	Heat generator seasonal efficiency (gross)	
		Thermal efficiency	Boiler seasonal efficiency
Direct-fired: new buildings	Natural gas > 30 kW output	90%	
	Natural gas ≤ 30 kW output	73%	
	LPG > 30 kW output	92%	
	LPG ≤ 30 kW output	74%	
	Oil	76%	
Direct-fired: existing buildings	Natural gas	73%	
	LPG	74%	
	Oil	75%	
Indirect-fired: new and existing buildings	Natural gas		80%
	LPG		81%
	Oil		82%
Electrically-heated: new and existing buildings		100% assumed	

Table 29 Recommended minimum controls package for gas and oil-fired domestic hot water systems

DHW system type	Controls package
Direct-fired circulator: natural gas and LPG	a. Automatic thermostat control to shut off the burner/primary heat supply when the desired temperature of the hot water has been reached. b. High limit thermostat to shut off primary flow if system temperature too high. c. Time control.
Direct-fired storage: natural gas, LPG and oil	a. Automatic thermostat control to shut off the burner/primary heat supply when the desired temperature of the hot water has been reached. b. High limit thermostat to shut off primary flow if system temperature too high. c. Time control.
Direct-fired continuous flow: natural gas and LPG	a. Outlet temperature of appliance controlled by rate of flow through heat exchanger. b. High limit thermostat to shut off primary flow if system temperature too high. c. Flow sensor that only allows electrical input should sufficient flow through the unit be achieved. d. Time control.
Indirect-fired: natural gas, LPG and oil	a. Automatic thermostat control to shut off the burner/primary heat supply when the desired temperature of the hot water has been reached. b. High limit thermostat to shut off primary flow if system temperature too high. c. Time control.

Table 30 Recommended minimum controls package for electrically-heated domestic hot water systems

	Point-of-use	Local	Centralised	Instantaneous
Automatic thermostat control to interrupt the electrical supply when the desired storage temperature has been reached.	Yes	Yes	Yes	x
High limit thermostat (thermal cut-out) to interrupt the energy supply if the system temperature gets too high.	Yes	Yes	Yes	x
Manual reset in the event of an over-temperature trip.	Yes	Yes	Yes	x
7-day time clock (or BMS interface) to ensure bulk heating of water using off-peak electricity. Facility to boost the temperature using on-peak electricity (ideally by means of an immersion heater fitted to heat the top 30% of the cylinder).	x	Yes	Yes	x
High limit thermostat (thermal cut-out) to interrupt the energy supply if the outlet temperature gets too high. (Note: Outlet temperature is controlled by rate of flow through the unit, which on basic units would be by the outlet tap or fitting.)	x	x	x	Yes
Flow/pressure sensor that only allows electrical input should sufficient flow through the unit be achieved.	x	x	x	Yes

8.5 Supplementary information on electric water heaters

Point-of-use

- Relevant standard is BS EN 60335-2-21:2003+A2:2008[33].

Instantaneous

- Relevant standard is BS EN 60335-2-35:2002+A2:2011[34].

Local

- For vented systems, relevant standard is BS EN 60335-2-21:2003+A2:2008.

- For unvented systems, relevant standard is BS EN 12897:2006[35].

Centralised

- Relevant standard is BS 853-1:1990+A3:2011[36].

- Bulk heating of the water should utilise off-peak electricity where possible.

- When using off-peak electricity a 'boost heater' should be fitted to allow 'on-peak' heating. The boost heater should heat the top 30% of the cylinder and be rated to approximately 30% of the main off-peak heater battery. The kW load will depend on the recovery time required.

---

33   BS EN 60335-2-21:2003+A2:2008 *Specification for safety of household and similar electrical appliances. Particular requirements for storage water heaters.*
34   BS EN 60335-2-35:2002+A2:2011 *Specification for safety of household and similar electrical appliances. Particular requirements for instantaneous water heaters.*
35   BS EN 12897:2006 *Water supply. Specification for indirectly heated unvented (closed) storage water heaters.*
36   BS 853-1:1990+A3:2011 *Calorifiers and storage vessels for central heating and hot water supplies.*

- The heater battery should either be of removable core or rod element construction. Removable core construction allows elements to be changed without removing the heater from the vessel or draining the system. For removable core construction, the maximum element watts density should not exceed 3 W/cm^2 for copper tubes or 2.5 W/cm^2 for stainless steel tubes. For rod element construction, elements should be of nickel alloy 825 sheath, be U-bent and have a maximum watts density of 10 W/cm^2. Temperature control should be by means of 'on/off' control of the heater battery utilising stage ramping for loadings above 30 kW. Thermostatic control is an ideal solution.

- The control sensor should be mounted in the cylinder at an angle of approximately 45° to the heater and at a level just above the heating bundle. The over-temperature sensor (high limit) should be mounted in the top 30% of the cylinder directly above the heater bundle. A manual reset should be required in the event of an over-temperature trip.

- For loadings greater than 6 kW, temperature sensors should not be fitted to the heater bundle. This is to prevent thermostat and contactor cycling which will lead to premature failure of the equipment and poor temperature control.

8.6 Heating efficiency credits for domestic hot water systems in new and existing buildings

Heating efficiency credits are available for gas and oil-fired systems for the additional measures listed in Table 31. If these measures are adopted, heating efficiency credits can be added to the heat generator seasonal efficiency to give the effective heat generator seasonal efficiency, which is the value entered into the accredited NCM tool in order to calculate the carbon dioxide emission rate for a building.

Effective heat generator seasonal efficiency = heat generator seasonal efficiency + heating efficiency credits

where the heat generator seasonal efficiency is:

- the thermal efficiency for direct-fired systems
- the boiler seasonal efficiency for indirect-fired systems.

Table 31 Heating efficiency credits for additional measures applicable to domestic hot water systems

System type	Measure	Heating efficiency credits (% points)
All	Decentralisation	2, but not applicable to systems in new buildings
Direct-fired	Integral combustion circuit shut-off device	1
	Fully automatic ignition controls	0.5
All	Correct size of unit confirmed using manufacturer's technical helpline and sizing software	2

Example: Using heating efficiency credits to improve the heat generator seasonal efficiency for a direct-fired circulator system

Step 1: Calculating thermal efficiency of direct-fired DHW system

- recovery rate of heater = 0.3830 litres/s
- gross input rate of heater = 83.5 kW
- specific heat capacity of water = 4.186 kJ/(kg·K)
- temperature rise of water inside heater = 50°C.

Using Equation 9:

Heater output = recovery rate of heater in litres/second × specific heat capacity of water × temperature rise of the water

= 0.3830 × 4.186 × 50 = 80.16 kW

Using Equation 8:

Thermal efficiency (gross) = output of the heater / gross input

= 80.16 / 83.5 = 0.96 (96%)

Step 2: Adding heating efficiency credits for additional measures

The heater has been sized to closely match the system demand by using the manufacturer's sizing guide and has fully automatic controls.

Table 32 shows how credits would be assigned in this example.

Table 32 Example to illustrate allocation of heating efficiency credits for a DHW system

Measure	Heating efficiency credits (% points)
Sized according to manufacturer's guidance	2
Fully automatic ignition controls	0.5
Total credits	**2.5**

Effective heat generator seasonal efficiency = thermal efficiency (gross) + heating efficiency credits

= 96 + 2.5 = 98.5%

In this example, the value 98.5% would be entered in the NCM tool.

Section 9: Comfort cooling

9.1 Introduction

This section gives guidance on specifying comfort cooling for new and existing buildings to meet relevant energy efficiency requirements in the Building Regulations. It includes guidance on using SBEM to calculate the carbon dioxide emissions associated with comfort cooling in new buildings.

9.2 Scope of guidance

The guidance covers the specification of refrigeration plant efficiency in terms of the seasonal energy efficiency ratio (SEER), which is the value used by SBEM to calculate the carbon dioxide emission rate for a new building. SBEM allocates standard correction factors[37] to the performance of cooling plant to account for the use of the different systems for distributing cooling to the spaces. Evaporative cooling and desiccant cooling systems are not within the scope of this guidance.

9.3 Key terms

Cooling plant means that part of a cooling system that produces the supply of cooling medium. It does not include means of distributing the cooling medium or the delivery of the cooling into the relevant zone. It may consist, for example, of a single chiller or a series of chillers.

Cooling system means the complete system that is installed to provide the comfort cooling to the space. It includes the cooling plant and the system by which the cooling medium effects cooling in the relevant zone and the associated controls. This will in some cases be a complete packaged air conditioner.

Energy efficiency ratio (EER) for chillers is the cooling energy delivered into the cooling system divided by the energy input to the chiller, as determined by BS EN 14511[38].

In the case of packaged air conditioners, the EER is the energy removed from air within the conditioned space divided by the effective energy input to the unit, as determined by BS EN 14511 or other appropriate standard procedure. The test conditions for determining EER are those specified in BS EN 14511.

Part load energy efficiency ratio is the cooling energy delivered into the cooling system divided by the energy input to the cooling plant. Part load performance for individual chillers is determined assuming chilled water provision at 7°C out and 12°C in (at 100% load), under the following conditions:

Percentage part load	25%	50%	75%	100%
Air-cooled chillers ambient air temperature (°C)	20	25	30	35
Water-cooled chillers entering cooling water temperature (°C)	18	22	26	30

Seasonal energy efficiency ratio (SEER) is the total amount of cooling energy provided divided by the total energy input to a single cooling unit, summed over the year.

---

37   The SBEM Technical Manual is available for download from www.ncm.bre.co.uk
38   BS EN 14511-2:2013 *Air conditioners, liquid chilling packages and heat pumps with electrically driven compressors for space heating and cooling. Test conditions.*

European Seasonal Energy Efficiency Ratio (ESEER) is the SEER of a cooling unit as determined under the Eurovent Certification scheme.

Plant seasonal energy efficiency ratio (PSEER) is the total amount of cooling energy provided divided by the total energy input to the cooling plant (which may comprise more than one cooling unit), summed over the year.

9.4 Comfort cooling in new and existing buildings

For comfort cooling systems in new and existing buildings:

a. cooling units should comply with European Commission Regulation No 327/2011 for fans driven by motors with an electrical input power between 125 W and 500 kW, and Regulation No 206/2012 for systems with a cooling capacity of up to 12 kW, both implementing Directive 2009/125/EC with regards to ecodesign requirements for energy-related products

b. the full load energy efficiency ratio (EER) of each cooling unit of the cooling plant should be no worse than recommended in Table 33

c. controls should comply with BS EN 15232:2012[39] Band C and be no worse than recommended in Table 34.

Table 33 Recommended minimum energy efficiency ratio (EER) for comfort cooling

Type		Cooling unit full load EER
Packaged air conditioners	Single-duct type	2.6
	Other types	2.6
Split and multi-split air conditioners > 12 kW		2.6
Split and multi-split air conditioners ≤ 12 kW		SCOP 'D' rating for median temperature range in BS EN 14825:2013[40]
Variable refrigerant flow systems		2.6
Vapour compression cycle chillers, water-cooled ≤ 750 kW		3.9
Vapour compression cycle chillers, water-cooled > 750 kW		4.7
Vapour compression cycle chillers, air-cooled ≤ 750 kW		2.55
Vapour compression cycle chillers, air-cooled > 750 kW		2.65
Water loop heat pump		3.2
Absorption cycle chillers		0.7
Gas-engine-driven variable refrigerant flow		1.0

39   BS EN 15232:2012 *Energy performance of buildings. Impact of building automation, controls and building management.*
40   BS EN 14825:2013 *Air conditioners, liquid chilling packages and heat pumps with electrically driven compressors for space heating and cooling. Testing and rating at part load conditions and calculation of seasonal performance.*

Table 34 Recommended minimum controls for comfort cooling in new and existing buildings

	Controls
Cooling plant	a. Multiple cooling units should be provided with controls that ensure the combined plant operates in its most efficient modes.
Cooling system	a. Terminal units capable of providing cooling should have integrated or remote time and temperature controls. b. In any given zone simultaneous heating and cooling should be prevented by an interlock.

9.5 Calculating the seasonal energy efficiency ratio for SBEM

The value of the SEER to be used in the SBEM tool can be calculated in a number of ways according to the availability of information and the application.

In general, where an industry approved test procedure for obtaining performance measurements of cooling units at partial load conditions exists, and the cooling load profile of the proposed building is known, the SEER of the cooling unit is given by:

$$SEER = a(EER_{100\%}) + b(EER_{75\%}) + c(EER_{50\%}) + d(EER_{25\%})$$ **Equation 10**

where:

EER_x is the EER measured at the load conditions of 100%, 75%, 50% and 25% at the operating conditions detailed under the part load energy efficiency ratio in Section 9.3

and:

a, b, c and d are the load profile weighting factors relevant to the proposed application.

The following sections describe how the SEER may be calculated for the specific cases of:

- cooling units with no part load performance data
- unknown load profiles
- office-type accommodation
- other buildings with known load profile data
- multiple-chiller systems
- systems with free cooling or heat recovery
- absorption chillers and district cooling.

Cooling units with no part load performance data

For cooling units that have no part load data, the SEER is the full load EER.

Unknown load profiles

For applications where the load profile under which the cooling plant operates is not known but there is some data on chiller part load EER, then:

a. for chillers where the full and half load (50%) EERs are known, the SEER is the average of the EERs, i.e. the 100% and 50% are equally weighted

b. for chillers with four points of part load EER, the SEER is calculated using Equation 10 with each EER weighted equally, i.e. a, b, c and d each equal to 0.25

c. if the chiller used does not have data for four steps of load, then the weights are apportioned appropriately.

Office-type accommodation

For applications in general office-type accommodation, the following weighting factors can be taken as representative of the load profile:

a	b	c	d
0.03	0.33	0.41	0.23

These weighting factors are the same as those used for the determination of the European Seasonal Energy Efficiency Ratio (ESEER). Most manufacturers publish ESEER figures and these can be verified by reference to the Eurovent Certification website at www.eurovent-certification.com. The ESEER value is then used as the SEER in the SBEM calculation.

Examples

1. For a single chiller with EER of 2.9 (known at full load only):

    $SEER = 2.9$

2. For a chiller with 100% and 50% EERs of 2.0 and 2.5 respectively in a building with unknown load profile:

    $SEER = 2.25$

3. For a chiller with unknown application load profile and part load EERs of $EER_{100\%} = 2.89$, $EER_{75\%} = 3.93$, $EER_{50\%} = 4.89$ and $EER_{25\%} = 4.79$:

    $SEER = 0.25 \times 2.89 + 0.25 \times 3.93 + 0.25 \times 4.89 + 0.25 \times 4.79 = 4.125$

4. If the same chiller is used in an office then the ESEER weighting factors are used:

    $SEER = ESEER = 0.03 \times 2.89 + 0.33 \times 3.93 + 0.41 \times 4.89 + 0.23 \times 4.79 = 4.49$

Other buildings with known load profile

If the load profile is known from detailed simulation or prediction, the SEER may be derived from Equation 10 above using appropriate weights and EERs at given loads.

Multiple-chiller systems

For plants with multiple-chillers, a plant seasonal energy efficiency ratio (PSEER) value may be calculated based on the sum of the energy consumptions of all the operating chillers. In this case care must be taken to include all the factors that can influence the combined performance of the multiple-chiller installation. These will include the:

*   degree of oversizing of the total installed capacity

*   sizes of individual chillers

*   EERs of individual chillers at actual operating conditions

*   control mode used: e.g. parallel, sequential, dedicated low load unit

*   load profile of the proposed building

*   building location (as this determines ambient conditions).

When these are known it may be possible to calculate a PSEER which matches the proposed installation more closely than by applying the simplifications described earlier. This PSEER value is then used as the SEER in the SBEM calculation.

Systems with free cooling or heat recovery

Systems that have the ability to use free cooling or heat recovery can achieve a greater SEER than more conventional systems. In these cases the SEER must be derived for the specific application under consideration.

Absorption chillers and district cooling

Absorption chillers may be used in conjunction with on-site CHP or a community or district heating system. The carbon dioxide emissions are calculated in the same way as when using CHP for heating. The control system should ensure as far as possible that heat from boilers is not used to supply the absorption chiller. The minimum full load EER of the absorption chillers should be no worse than 0.7.

Where a district cooling scheme exists, lower carbon dioxide emissions may result if the cooling is produced centrally from CHP/absorption chillers, heat pumps or high efficiency vapour compression chillers. The district cooling company will provide information on the carbon dioxide content of the cooling energy supplied, and this figure can then be used to calculate the carbon dioxide emission rate for the building.

9.6 Supplementary information

BS EN 15243:2007[41] provides additional guidance on calculating the seasonal efficiency of cold generators and chillers in air conditioning systems. The guidance does not need to be followed to meet relevant energy efficiency requirements in the Building Regulations.

---

41   BS EN 15243:2007 *Ventilation for buildings. Calculation of room temperatures and of load and energy for buildings with room conditioning systems.*

Section 10: Air distribution

10.1 Introduction

This section gives guidance on specifying air distribution systems for new and existing buildings to meet relevant energy efficiency requirements in the Building Regulations.

10.2 Scope of guidance

The guidance applies to the following types of air distribution system:

- central air conditioning systems

- central mechanical ventilation systems with heating, cooling or heat recovery

- all central systems not covered by the above two types

- zonal supply systems where the fan is remote from the zone, such as ceiling void or roof-mounted units

- zonal extract systems where the fan is remote from the zone

- local supply and extract ventilation units such as window, wall or roof units serving a single area (e.g. toilet extract)

- other local ventilation units, e.g. fan coil units and fan assisted terminal variable air volume (VAV) units

- kitchen extract, fan remote from zone with grease filter.

Gas and oil-fired air heaters installed within the area to be heated are not within the scope of this section.

10.3 Key terms

Air conditioning system means a combination of components required to provide a form of air treatment in which temperature is controlled or can be lowered, possibly in combination with the control of ventilation, humidity and air cleanliness.

Ventilation system means a combination of components required to provide air treatment in which temperature, ventilation and air cleanliness are controlled.

Central system means a supply and extract system which serves the whole or major zones of the building.

Local unit means an unducted ventilation unit serving a single area.

Zonal system means a system which serves a group of rooms forming part of a building, i.e. a zone where ducting is required.

Demand control is a type of control where the ventilation rate is controlled by air quality, moisture, occupancy or some other indicator of the need for ventilation.

Specific fan power (SFP) of an air distribution system means the sum of the design circuit-watts of the system fans that supply air and exhaust it back outdoors, including losses through switchgear and controls such as inverters (i.e. the total circuit-watts for the supply and extract fans), divided by the design air flow rate through that system.

For the purposes of this guide, the specific fan power of an air distribution system should be calculated according to the procedure set out in BS EN 13779:2007[42] Annex D *Calculation and application of specific fan power. Calculating and checking the SFP, SFP$_E$ and SFP$_V$.*

$$\text{SFP} = \frac{P_{sf} + P_{ef}}{q}$$

Equation 11

where:

SFP is the specific fan power demand of the air distribution system (W/(l·s))

P_{sf} is the total fan power of all supply air fans at the design air flow rate, including power losses through switchgear and controls associated with powering and controlling the fans (W)

P_{ef} is the total fan power of all exhaust air fans at the design air flow rate including power losses through switchgear and controls associated with powering and controlling the fans (W)

q is the design air flow rate through the system, which should be the greater of either the supply or exhaust air flow (l/s). Note that for an air handling unit, q is the largest supply or extract air flow through the unit.

External system pressure drop means the total system pressure drop excluding the pressure drop across the air handling unit.

10.4 Air distribution systems in new and existing buildings

Air distribution systems in new and existing buildings should meet the following recommended minimum standards:

a. Air handling systems should be capable of achieving a specific fan power at 25% of design flow rate no greater than that achieved at 100% design flow rate.

b. In order to aid commissioning and to provide flexibility for future changes of use, reasonable provision would be to equip with variable speed drives those fans that are rated at more than 1100 W and which form part of the environmental control systems, including smoke control fans used for control of overheating. The provision is not applicable to smoke control fans and similar ventilation systems only used in abnormal circumstances.

---

42   BS EN 13779:2007 *Ventilation for non-residential buildings. Performance requirements for ventilation and room-conditioning systems.*

c. In order to limit air leakage, ventilation ductwork should be made and assembled so as to be reasonably airtight. Ways of meeting this requirement would be to comply with the specifications given in:

    i. B&ES DW/144[43]. Membership of the B&ES specialist ductwork group or the Association of Ductwork Contractors and Allied Services is one way of demonstrating suitable qualifications, or

    ii. British Standards such as BS EN 1507:2006[44], BS EN 12237:2003[45] and BS EN 13403:2003[46].

d. In order to limit air leakage, air handling units should be made and assembled so as to be reasonably airtight. Ways of meeting this requirement would be to comply with Class L2 air leakage given in BS EN 1886:2007[47].

e. The specific fan power of air distribution systems at the design air flow rate should be no worse than in Table 35 for new and existing buildings. Specific fan power is a function of the system resistance that the fan has to overcome to provide the required flow rate. BS EN 13779 Table A8 provides guidance on system pressure drop. To minimise specific fan power it is recommended that the 'low range' is used as a design target.

f. Where the primary air and cooling is provided by central plant and by an air distribution system that includes the additional components listed in Table 36, the allowed specific fan powers may be increased by the amounts shown in Table 36 to account for the additional resistance.

g. A minimum controls package should be provided in new and existing buildings as in Table 37.

h. Ventilation fans driven by electric motors should comply with European Commission Regulation No 327/2011 implementing Directive 2009/125/EC with regard to ecodesign requirements for fans driven by motors with an electric input power between 125 W and 500 kW.

43   Ductwork Specification DW/144 *Specifications for sheet metal ductwork. Low, medium and high pressure/velocity air system*, B&ES, 2013.
44   BS EN 1507:2006 *Ventilation for buildings. Sheet metal air ducts with rectangular section. Requirements for strength and leakage.*
45   BS EN 12237:2003 *Ventilation for buildings. Ductwork. Strength and leakage of circular sheet metal ducts.*
46   BS EN 13403:2003 *Ventilation for buildings. Non-metallic ducts. Ductwork made from insulation ductboards.*
47   BS EN 1886:2007 *Ventilation for buildings. Air handling units. Mechanical performance.*

Table 35 Maximum specific fan power in air distribution systems in new and existing buildings

System type	SFP (W/(l·s))	
	New buildings	Existing buildings
Central balanced mechanical ventilation system with heating and cooling	1.6	2.2
Central balanced mechanical ventilation system with heating only	1.5	1.8
All other central balanced mechanical ventilation systems	1.1	1.6
Zonal supply system where fan is remote from zone, such as ceiling void or roof-mounted units	1.1	1.4
Zonal extract system where fan is remote from zone	0.5	0.5
Zonal supply and extract ventilation units, such as ceiling void or roof units serving single room or zone with heating and heat recovery	1.9	1.9
Local balanced supply and extract ventilation system such as wall/roof units serving single area with heat recovery	1.6	1.6
Local supply or extract ventilation units such as window/wall/roof units serving single area (e.g. toilet extract)	0.3	0.4
Other local ventilation supply or extract units	0.5	0.5
Fan assisted terminal VAV unit	1.1	1.1
Fan coil unit (rating weighted average*)	0.5	0.5
Kitchen extract, fan remote from zone with grease filter	1.0	1.0

* The rating weighted average is calculated by the following formula:

$$\frac{P_{mains,1} \times SFP_1 + P_{mains,2} \times SFP_2 + P_{mains,3} \times SFP_3 + \dots}{P_{mains,1} + P_{mains,2} + P_{mains,3} + \dots}$$

where P_{mains} is useful power supplied from the mains in W.

Table 36 Extending specific fan power for additional components in new and existing buildings

Component	SFP (W/(l·s))
Additional return filter for heat recovery	+0.1
HEPA filter	+1.0
Heat recovery – thermal wheel system	+0.3
Heat recovery – other systems	+0.3
Humidifier/dehumidifier (air conditioning system)	+0.1

Example:

For a central mechanical ventilation system with heating and cooling, and heat recovery via a plate heat exchanger plus return filter:

SFP $\quad = 1.6 + 0.3 + 0.1$ W/(l·s)

$\quad\quad = 2.0$ W/(l·s)

Table 37 Recommended minimum controls for air distribution systems in new and existing buildings from BS EN 15232:2012[48]

System type		Controls package
Central mechanical ventilation with heating, cooling or heat recovery	Air flow control at room level	Time control
	Air flow control at air handler level	On/off time control
	Heat exchanger defrosting control	Defrost control so that during cold periods ice does not form on the heat exchanger
	Heat exchanger overheating control	Overheating control so that when the system is cooling and heat recovery is undesirable, the heat exchanger is stopped, modulated or bypassed
	Supply temperature control	Variable set point with outdoor temperature compensation
Central mechanical ventilation with heating or heat recovery	Air flow control at room level	Time control
	Air flow control at air handler level	On/off time control
	Heat exchanger defrosting control	Defrost control so that during cold periods ice does not form on the heat exchanger
	Heat exchanger overheating control	Overheating control so that when the system is cooling and heat recovery is undesirable, the heat exchanger is stopped, modulated or bypassed
	Supply temperature control	Demand control
Zonal	Air flow control at room level	On/off time control
	Air flow control at air handler level	No control
	Supply temperature control	No control
Local	Air flow control at room level	On/off
	Air flow control at air handler level	No control
	Supply temperature control	No control

---

48   BS EN 15232:2012 *Energy performance of buildings. Impact of building automation, controls and building management.*

10.5 Heat recovery in air distribution systems in new and existing buildings

Air supply and extract ventilation systems including heating or cooling should be fitted with a heat recovery system. The application of a heat recovery system is described in 6.5 of BS EN 13053:2006+A1:2011[49]. The methods for testing air-to-air heat recovery devices are given in BS EN 308:1997[50].

The minimum dry heat recovery efficiency with reference to the mass flow ratio 1:1 should be no less than that recommended in Table 38.

Table 38 Recommended minimum dry heat recovery efficiency for heat exchangers in new and existing buildings

Heat exchanger type	Dry heat recovery efficiency (%)
Plate heat exchanger	50
Heat pipes	60
Thermal wheel	65
Run around coil	45

10.6 Calculating the specific fan power for SBEM

SBEM assumes a value of SFP for the fan coil system, so this figure should not be added to the SFP for the fan coil units when entering the data into SBEM.

HEPA filtration is recognised as an option in SBEM. The pressure drop can be specified or SBEM will assume a default value from the NCM activity database.

---

49   BS EN 13053:2006+A1:2011 *Ventilation for buildings. Air handling units. Rating and performance for units, components and sections.*
50   BS EN 308:1997 *Heat exchangers. Test procedures for establishing the performance of air to air and flue gases heat recovery devices.*

Section 11: Pipework and ductwork insulation

11.1 Introduction

This section gives guidance on insulating pipework and ducting serving space heating, hot water and cooling systems in new and existing buildings to meet relevant energy efficiency requirements in the Building Regulations.

The insulation of pipework and ducting is essential to minimise heating system heat losses and cooling system heat gains. For cooling systems, it is also important to ensure that the risk of condensation is adequately controlled.

11.2 Scope of guidance

The guidance in this section covers insulation for the following types of pipework and ductwork serving space heating, domestic hot water and cooling systems:

- pipework: direct hot water, low, medium and high temperature heating, and cooled

- ductwork: heated, cooled and dual-purpose heated and cooled.

11.3 Insulation of pipes and ducts in new and existing buildings

Insulation of pipes and ducts serving heating and cooling systems should meet the following recommended minimum standards. The relevant standard for calculating insulation thickness is BS EN ISO 12241:2008[51].

a. **Direct hot water and heating pipework**

   i. Pipework serving space heating and hot water systems should be insulated in all areas outside of the heated building envelope. In addition, pipes should be insulated in all voids within the building envelope and within spaces which will normally be heated, if there is a possibility that those spaces might be maintained at temperatures different to those maintained in other zones. The guiding principles are that control should be maximised and that heat loss from uninsulated pipes should only be permitted where the heat can be demonstrated as 'always useful'.

   ii. In order to demonstrate compliance, the heat losses shown in Table 39 for different pipe sizes and temperatures should not be exceeded.

b. **Cooling pipework**

   i. Cooling pipework should be insulated along its whole length in order to provide the necessary means of limiting heat gain. Control should be maximised and heat gain to uninsulated pipes should only be permitted where the proportion of the cooling load relating to distribution pipework is proven to be less than 1% of total load.

   ii. In order to demonstrate compliance, the heat gains in Table 40 for different pipe sizes and temperatures should not be exceeded.

   iii. Although unrelated to meeting relevant energy efficiency requirements in the Building Regulations, provision should also be made for control of condensation by following TIMSA guidance[52].

---

51 BS EN ISO 12241:2008. *Thermal insulation for building equipment and industrial installations. Calculation rules.*
52 TIMSA *HVAC guidance for achieving compliance with Part L of the Building Regulations.*

c. Heating and cooling ductwork

i. Ducting should be insulated along its whole length in order to provide the necessary means of limiting heat gains or heat losses.

ii. The heat losses or gains per unit area should not exceed the values in Table 41. Where ducting may be used for both heating and cooling, the limits for chilled ducting should be adopted since these are more onerous. (Heat gains are shown as negative values.)

iii. As with pipework, additional insulation may be required to provide adequate condensation control, as detailed in TIMSA guidance.

Table 39 Recommended maximum heat losses for direct hot water and heating pipes

Outside pipe diameter (mm)	Heat loss (W/m)			
	Hot water[1]	Low temperature heating[2]	Medium temperature heating[3]	High temperature heating[4]
		≤ 95°C	96°C to 120°C	121°C to 150°C
17.2	6.60	8.90	13.34	17.92
21.3	7.13	9.28	13.56	18.32
26.9	7.83	10.06	13.83	18.70
33.7	8.62	11.07	14.39	19.02
42.4	9.72	12.30	15.66	19.25
48.3	10.21	12.94	16.67	20.17
60.3	11.57	14.45	18.25	21.96
76.1	13.09	16.35	20.42	24.21
88.9	14.58	17.91	22.09	25.99
114.3	17.20	20.77	25.31	29.32
139.7	19.65	23.71	28.23	32.47
168.3	22.31	26.89	31.61	36.04
219.1	27.52	32.54	37.66	42.16
≥ 273.0	32.40	38.83	43.72	48.48

Note
To ensure compliance with the maximum heat loss criteria, insulation thicknesses should be calculated according to BS EN ISO 12241 using standardised assumptions:
[1] Horizontal pipe at 60°C in still air at 15°C
[2] Horizontal pipe at 75°C in still air at 15°C
[3] Horizontal pipe at 100°C in still air at 15°C
[4] Horizontal pipe at 125°C in still air at 15°C

Table 40 Recommended maximum heat gains for cooled water supply pipes

Outside diameter of steel pipe on which insulation has been based (mm)	Heat gain (W/m)		
	Temperature of contents (°C)		
	>10[1]	4.9 to 10.0[2]	0 to 4.9[3]
17.2	2.48	2.97	3.47
21.3	2.72	3.27	3.81
26.9	3.05	3.58	4.18
33.7	3.41	4.01	4.60
42.4	3.86	4.53	5.11
48.3	4.11	4.82	5.45
60.3	4.78	5.48	6.17
76.1	5.51	6.30	6.70
88.9	6.17	6.90	7.77
114.3	7.28	8.31	9.15
139.7	8.52	9.49	10.45
168.3	9.89	10.97	11.86
219.1	12.27	13.57	14.61
≥273.0	14.74	16.28	17.48

Note
To ensure compliance with the maximum heat gain criteria, insulation thicknesses should be calculated according to BS EN ISO 12241 using standardised assumptions:
[1]   Horizontal pipe at 10°C in still air at 25°C
[2]   Horizontal pipe at 5°C in still air at 25°C
[3]   Horizontal pipe at 0°C in still air at 25°C

Table 41 Recommended maximum heat losses and gains for insulated heating, cooling and dual-purpose ducts

	Heating duct[1]	Dual-purpose duct[2]	Cooling duct[3]
Heat transfer (W/m²)	16.34	-6.45	-6.45

Note
To ensure compliance with maximum heat transfer criteria, insulation thicknesses should be calculated according to BS EN ISO 12241 using standardised assumptions:
[1]   Horizontal duct at 35°C, with 600 mm vertical sidewall in still air at 15°C
[2]   Horizontal duct at 13°C, with 600 mm vertical sidewall in still air at 25°C
[3]   Horizontal duct at 13°C, with 600 mm vertical sidewall in still air at 25°C

Section 12: Lighting

12.1 Introduction

This section provides guidance on specifying lighting for new and existing non-domestic buildings to meet relevant energy efficiency requirements in the Building Regulations. There are two alternative approaches, applicable both to systems in new buildings and to replacement systems in existing buildings.

12.2 Scope of guidance

The guidance in this section applies to the following types of lighting:

- general interior lighting

- display lighting.

12.3 Key terms

Office area means a space that involves predominantly desk-based tasks – e.g. a classroom, seminar or conference room.

Daylit space means any space:

a. within 6 m of a window wall, provided that the glazing area is at least 20% of the internal area of the window wall

b. below rooflights, provided that the glazing area is at least 10% of the floor area.

The normal light transmittance of the glazing should be at least 70%; if the light transmittance is below 70%, the glazing area should be increased proportionately for the space to be defined as daylit.

Space classification for control purposes[53]:

Owned space means a space such as a small room for one or two people who control the lighting – e.g. a cellular office or consulting room.

Shared space means a multi-occupied area – e.g. an open-plan office or factory production area.

Temporarily owned space means a space where people are expected to operate the lighting controls while they are there – e.g. a hotel room or meeting room.

Occasionally visited space means a space where people generally stay for a relatively short period of time when they visit the space – e.g. a storeroom or toilet.

Unowned space means a space where individual users require lighting but are not expected to operate the lighting controls – e.g. a corridor or atrium.

Managed space means a space where lighting is under the control of a responsible person – e.g. a hotel lounge, restaurant or shop.

Local manual switching means that the distance on plan from any local switch to the luminaire it controls should generally be not more than 6 m, or twice the height of the light fitting above the floor if this is greater. Where the space is a daylit space served by side windows, the perimeter row of lighting should in general be separately switched.

---

53   These definitions are given in more detail in BRE Information Paper IP6/96 *People and lighting controls* and BRE Digest 498 *Selecting lighting controls.*

Photoelectric control is a type of control which switches or dims lighting in response to the amount of incoming daylight.

Presence detection is a type of control which switches the lighting on when someone enters a space, and switches it off, or dims it down, after the space becomes unoccupied.

Absence detection is a type of control which switches the lighting off, or dims it down, after the space becomes unoccupied, but where switching on is done manually.

Lamp lumens means the sum of the average initial (100 hour) lumen output of all the lamps in the luminaire.

Circuit-watt is the power consumed in lighting circuits by lamps and, where applicable, their associated control gear (including transformers and drivers) and power factor correction equipment.

Lamp lumens per circuit-watt is the total lamp lumens summed for all luminaires in the relevant areas of the building, divided by the total circuit-watts for all the luminaires.

LOR is the light output ratio of the luminaire, which means the ratio of the total light output of the luminaire under stated practical conditions to that of the lamp or lamps contained in the luminaire under reference conditions.

Luminaire lumens per circuit-watt is the (lamp lumens $\times$ LOR) summed for all luminaires in the relevant areas of the building, divided by the total circuit-watts for all the luminaires.

LENI (Lighting Energy Numeric Indicator) is a measure of the performance of lighting in terms of energy per square metre per year ($kWh/m^2/year$), based on BS EN 15193:2007 *Energy performance of buildings. Energy requirements for lighting*.

12.4 Lighting in new and existing buildings

a.   Lighting in new and existing buildings should meet the recommended minimum standards for:

i.   efficacy (averaged over the whole area of the applicable type of space in the building) and controls in Table 42

OR

ii.   the LENI in Table 44. The LENI should be calculated using the procedure described in Section 12.5.

b.   The lighting should be metered to record its energy consumption in accordance with the minimum standards in Table 43.

c.   Lighting controls in new and existing buildings should follow the guidance in BRE Digest 498 *Selecting lighting controls*. Display lighting, where provided, should be controlled on dedicated circuits that can be switched off at times when people will not be inspecting exhibits or merchandise, or being entertained.

Table 42 Recommended minimum lighting efficacy with controls in new and existing buildings

General lighting in office, industrial and storage spaces		Initial luminaire lumens/circuit-watt
		60
Controls	Control factor	Reduced luminaire lumens/circuit-watt
a daylit space with photo-switching with or without override	0.90	54
b daylit space with photo-switching and dimming with or without override	0.85	51
c unoccupied space with auto on and off	0.90	54
d unoccupied space with manual on and auto off	0.85	51
e space not daylit, dimmed for constant illuminance	0.90	54
a + c	0.80	48
a + d	0.75	45
b + c	0.75	45
b + d	0.70	42
e + c	0.80	48
e + d	0.75	45
General lighting in other types of space		The average initial efficacy should be not less than 60 lamp lumens per circuit-watt
Display lighting		The average initial efficacy should be not less than 22 lamp lumens per circuit-watt

Table 43 Recommended minimum standards for metering of general and display lighting in new and existing buildings

	Standard
Metering for general or display lighting	a. kWh meters on dedicated lighting circuits in the electrical distribution, or b. local power meter coupled to or integrated in the lighting controllers of a lighting or building management system, or c. a lighting management system that can calculate the consumed energy and make this information available to a building management system or in an exportable file format. (This could involve logging the hours run and the dimming level, and relating this to the installed load.)

12.5 Lighting Energy Numeric Indicator (LENI)

An alternative to complying with the efficacy standards in Table 42 is to follow the Lighting Energy Numeric Indicator (LENI) method.

The LENI method calculates the performance of lighting in terms of energy per square metre per year. The approach described below must be followed in calculating the LENI for a lighting scheme. The LENI should not exceed the lighting energy limit specified in Table 44 for a given illuminance and hours run.

Design the lighting

The first step to energy efficient lighting is to design the lighting installation in a way that meets all of the users' needs for the space under consideration. Recommendations for appropriate illuminance values and other lighting requirements may be found in BS EN 12464-1:2011[54], and in the Society of Light and Lighting (SLL) *Code for Lighting. The SLL Lighting Handbook* provides practical advice on how to design lighting for a number of different applications[55].

Look up the lighting energy limit

In designing the lighting, a level of illuminance will have been selected as necessary for the tasks being done in a particular area. It is also necessary to determine how many hours per year the lighting will be needed. Once both the illuminance and the hours are known it is possible to look up the lighting energy limit in Table 44. For example, a classroom in a school may be lit to 300 lux and used for 40 hours per week for 39 weeks of the year, giving a total of 1560 hours per year. Values of 1500 hours and 300 lux give a lighting energy limit of 7.70. Table 44 also gives day-time (T_d) and night-time (T_n) hour values which are used in the calculation of energy consumption.

If display lighting is used, then the lighting energy limit may be increased by the value given for normal display lighting for the area of the room where display lighting is used. For example, in an entrance area for a building there may be some display lighting in a small area around the reception desk but not in the rest of the area.

Shop windows use a lot of display lighting and may use up to 192.72 kWh/m²/year if the window faces a public road, and 96.8 kWh/m²/year if the window is in a shopping centre that is closed during the night.

Calculate the parasitic energy use (E_p)

If some form of lighting control system is used, then an allowance needs to be made for the energy used by the control system, and the fact that the luminaires take a little power even if they are dimmed down to give no light. An allowance of 0.3 W/m² should be made for power used in this way. If the whole lighting system is switched off when the room is not in use, then the power loss is only during the hours of use. If the system is left on all the time then the power loss occurs for 8760 hours per year.

If no lighting control system is used, then the parasitic energy use is zero.

Determine the total power of lighting (P_l)

This is the total power in watts consumed by the luminaires within a space.

---

54   BS EN 12464-1:2011. *Light and lighting. Lighting of work places. Indoor work places.*
55   For further information, see www.sll.org.uk and www.thelia.org.uk.

Determine the occupancy factor (F_o)

F_o allows for the fact that energy is saved if an automatic control system detects the presence or absence of people in a room and switches off the lights when there is nobody using the room. If no automatic control is used, then the occupancy factor $F_o = 1$. If controls turn off the lights within 20 minutes of the room being empty, then $F_o = 0.8$.

Determine the factor for daylight (F_d)

F_d allows for the fact that if the lighting is dimmed down when there is daylight available, then less energy will be used. If no daylight-linked dimming system is used, then $F_d = 1$. If the electric lighting dims in response to daylight being available, then in areas with adequate daylight $F_d = 0.8$. Adequate daylight may be found in areas that are within 6 m of a window wall or in areas where 10% or more of the roof is translucent or made up of rooflights.

Determine the constant illuminance factor (F_c)

When lighting is designed, a maintenance factor (MF) is used to allow for the fact that as the lighting system ages it produces less light. This means that on day one the lighting system is providing more light than needed. Thus with a constant illuminance system, it is possible to under-run the lighting on day one, and then slowly increase the power used by the lighting until the point is reached when maintenance needs to be carried out by changing the lamps or cleaning the luminaires. Systems that control the lighting in this way have an $F_c = 0.9$, and those that do not have an $F_c = 1$.

Calculate the daytime energy use (E_d)

The daytime energy use is:

$$E_d = \frac{P_l \times F_o \times F_d \times F_c \times T_d}{1000}$$

Calculate the night-time energy use (E_n)

The night-time energy use is:

$$E_n = \frac{P_l \times F_o \times F_c \times T_n}{1000}$$

Calculate total energy (kWh) per square metre per year (LENI)

The total energy per square metre per year is the sum of the daytime, night-time and parasitic energy uses per year divided by the area (A), as set out in the formula below:

$$LENI = \frac{E_p + E_d + E_n}{A}$$

Table 44 Recommended maximum LENI (kWh per square metre per year) in new and existing buildings

Hours			Illuminance (lux)								Display lighting	
Total	Day	Night	50	100	150	200	300	500	750	1000	Normal	Shop window
1000	821	179	1.11	1.92	2.73	3.54	5.17	8.41	12.47	16.52	10.00	
1500	1277	223	1.66	2.87	4.07	5.28	7.70	12.53	18.57	24.62	15.00	
2000	1726	274	2.21	3.81	5.42	7.03	10.24	16.67	24.70	32.73	20.00	
2500	2164	336	2.76	4.76	6.77	8.78	12.79	20.82	30.86	40.89	25.00	
3000	2585	415	3.31	5.72	8.13	10.54	15.37	25.01	37.06	49.12	30.00	
3700	3133	567	4.09	7.08	10.06	13.04	19.01	30.95	45.87	60.78	37.00	
4400	3621	779	4.89	8.46	12.02	15.59	22.73	37.00	54.84	72.68	44.00	96.80
5400	4184	1216	6.05	10.47	14.90	19.33	28.18	45.89	68.03	90.17	54.00	
6400	4547	1853	7.24	12.57	17.89	23.22	33.87	55.16	81.79	108.41	64.00	
8760	4380	4380	10.26	17.89	25.53	33.16	48.43	78.96	117.12	155.29	87.60	192.72

Section 13: Heating and cooling system circulators and water pumps

13.1 Introduction

Heating and cooling water in HVAC systems of non-domestic buildings can circulate for extensive periods and be responsible for considerable energy use.

13.2 Scope of guidance

This section provides guidance on specifying:

- heating system glandless circulators, both standalone and integrated in products
- heating and cooling system water pumps

to limit their energy consumption and meet relevant energy efficiency requirements in the Building Regulations. The guidance covers circulators and water pumps when used in closed systems.

13.3 Key terms

Heating system glandless circulator means a pump used to circulate hot water in closed circuit heating systems. The glandless (or wet rotor) circulator is a centrifugal pump with an integral motor and no mechanical seal. It can have an integrated motor drive unit for variable speed operation.

Water pump (also known as 'dry rotor' or 'direct coupled' pump) means a centrifugal pump driven by an electric motor and generally having mechanical seals. Common pump types include in-line, end suction and vertical multi-stage. The first two are usually single-stage pumps having single-entry volute. By design they can all be used as circulators for all HVAC applications depending on configuration and duty.

13.4 Glandless circulators and water pumps in new and existing buildings

Heating system glandless circulators and heating and cooling system water pumps in new and existing buildings should meet the recommended minimum standards in Table 45.

Table 45 Recommended minimum standards for heating system glandless circulators and heating and cooling system water pumps in new and existing buildings

a. In accordance with European Commission Regulation No 622/2012 (amending 641/2009) implementing Directive 2009/125/EC with regard to ecodesign requirements for glandless circulators up to 2.5 kW:

    i. From 1 January 2013, standalone glandless circulators, other than those specifically designed for primary circuits of thermal solar systems and of heat pumps, should have an Energy Efficiency Index (EEI) no greater than 0.27.

    ii. From 1 August 2015, standalone glandless circulators and glandless circulators integrated in products should have an Energy Efficiency Index (EEI) no greater than 0.23.

b. Variable speed glandless circulators should be used on variable volume systems.

c. Water pumps should comply with the requirements of European Commission Regulation No 547/2012 implementing Directive 2009/125/EC with regard to ecodesign requirements for water pumps.

d. If a water pump is used on a closed loop circuit and the motor is rated at more than 750 W, then it should be fitted with or controlled by an appropriate variable speed controller on any variable volume system. On water pump booster sets with an open loop circuit, the static head should be checked before an appropriate variable speed controller is used.

13.5 Supplementary information

Further information and guidance is available from www.bpma.org.uk where a list of approved glandless circulators and water pumps can be found.

Appendix A: Abbreviations

BER	Building carbon dioxide emission rate
BMS	Building management system
BS	British Standard
CHP	Combined heat and power
CHPQA	Combined Heat and Power Quality Assurance
CO_2	Carbon dioxide
COP	Coefficient of performance
DCLG	Department for Communities and Local Government
DECC	Department of Energy and Climate Change
DHW	Domestic hot water
EEI	Energy Efficiency Index
EER	Energy efficiency ratio
EN	European Norm (standard)
ESEER	European Seasonal Energy Efficiency Ratio
HEPA	High-efficiency particulate absorption
HVAC	Heating, ventilation and air conditioning
LENI	Lighting Energy Numeric Indicator
LPG	Liquified petroleum gas
MF	Maintenance factor
NCM	National Calculation Methodology
PSEER	Plant seasonal energy efficiency ratio
QI	Quality index
RHI	Renewable Heat Incentive
SAP	Standard Assessment Procedure
SBEM	Simplified Building Energy Model
SCOP	Seasonal coefficient of performance
SEER	Seasonal energy efficiency ratio
SFP	Specific fan power
SI	Statutory Instrument
SPEER	Seasonal primary energy efficiency ratio
SPF	Seasonal performance factor
TER	Target carbon dioxide emission rate
TRV	Thermostatic radiator valve
VAV	Variable air volume